WIT

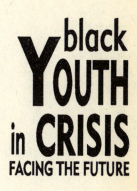

black
YOUTH
in CRISIS
FACING THE FUTURE

black Youth in CRISIS

FACING THE FUTURE

Edited for CASE by
David Everatt and Elinor Sisulu

Ravan Press

Published by Ravan Press Pty (Ltd)
P O Box 31134, Braamfontein, 2017, South Africa

First impression 1992
Second impression 1992

ISBN 0 86975 429 7

DTP setting by Ravan Press

Cover photograph by Paul Weinberg

Printed and bound by Sigma Press (Pty) Ltd, Pretoria

Contents

Acknowledgements

The editors would like to thank a number of people for their assistance in the preparation of this volume. Firstly Sheila Sisulu, Director of the Joint Enrichment Project, whose determination brought the entire marginalised youth programme into being, and who somehow remained calm when all about her were in panic.

Secondly, the staff of CASE all provided inputs and assistance. In particular, Nobayeti Dube assisted with typing while Susan Milner found the facts and figures necessary to update the texts. The authors also bore our requests and demands with remarkable patience.

Finally, our thanks go to Professor Mark Orkin, Director of CASE, who brought to the project his characteristic energy and vision, as well as formidable critical and editing skills.

Foreword

Sheila Sisulu
Director, Joint Enrichment Project

During the 1980s South Africa's schools became battlegrounds where young people waged war against the brutality of the apartheid system.

'Liberation before Education' echoed through the empty schools, a defiant battle cry that symbolised the sacrifices youth were forced to make.

Concerned that the culture of learning would be completely destroyed in the necessary onslaught against bantu education, the South African Council of Churches (SACC) and the South African Catholic Bishops Conference (SACBC) established the Joint Enrichment Project (JEP). The JEP provided creative skills programmes in art, drama and music which enabled students to tap deeper resources and build the self-confidence negatively affected by bantu education.

By 1990 a 'Back to School' campaign had been launched and students were supposedly returning to the classrooms. It became increasingly obvious, however, that large numbers of young people had slipped through the cracks in the transition period. Many youths who are now marginalised are not in schools, they are not in training institutions, they are not in employment. They are frequently referred to dismissively as the 'lost generation', the sacrifice South Africa sadly had to make.

The term 'lost generation' is negative, defeatist and fundamentally wrong. The youth are not 'lost' nor 'misplaced': they are present in increasing numbers and being marginalised from society. Marginalisation is not a necessary condition of youth: it is a problem of society which society must begin to address. Every person, every organisation, every corporation must begin to ask how to address the issue of marginalised youth.

It was with the aim of placing marginalised youth on the national agenda that the JEP convened the Broederstroom Conference. More than 300 representatives from over 50 national organisations were invited to debate and gain a critical understanding of the problems facing youth and the implications these hold for society. The JEP was then mandated to take forward the conference recommendations under the guidance of a joint SACC and SACBC working group.

The JEP has been undertaking this work, the results of which will be presented and discussed at a report back conference in late 1992.

The contributions contained in this book present a clear picture of the magnitude and complexity of the problems facing marginalised youth. Our responsibility is to respond to these.

Every sector is able to offer unique insights and means of providing a solution to marginalisation. We beseech all who read this book to do so in a critical manner, and to constantly ask the question: 'In my personal capacity, at work, at leisure – what are the practical ways in which I can respond?'

CASE

The Community Agency for Social Enquiry (CASE) is an independent research and training resource which has serviced the progressive movement since 1986.

CASE has undertaken national policy research for organisations including the South African Council of Churches, the South African Catholic Bishops Conference, the Nederduitse Gereformeerde Kerk (Afrika), the Congress of South African Trade Unions (Cosatu), the South African Committee for Higher Education (Sached), and a host of others. CASE also undertakes computer training for progressive organisations, operating from its offices in Johannesburg, Cape Town and Pietermaritzburg.

In regard to the JEP, CASE provided the research co-ordination for the conference on 'Marginalised Youth' organised by the Joint Enrichment Project (JEP) in June 1991. In September 1991, CASE was commissioned by the JEP to design and implement a major research project as an integral part of the National Youth Development Programme which flowed from the 'Marginalised Youth' conference.

The CASE research programme has the following elements:

♦ *Local research database and resource centre:* researchers have been collecting research into youth and youth-related issues from all over South Africa. The material is catalogued and databased in a user-friendly Resource centre which will be housed by the JEP.

♦ *National survey*: a national baseline survey will sample youth in all their diversity and allow them to express their own views on their needs, the problems they face, and how effective solutions can be arrived at.

♦ *International comparative data:* researchers have visited Botswana, Uganda, and Kenya to study youth development as it is taking place in Africa. This includes youth brigades, job creation schemes, AIDS awareness campaigns, and more. Further comparative data may be drawn from central America. Researchers also visited Geneva and London to liaise with and learn from the International Labour Organisation, World Health Organisation, United Nations, the Commonwealth Secretariat and others.

♦ *Publications:* all of the above research will be made public. Reports of the databased local research into youth and AIDS, education, the economy and job creation, violence and social context, as well as an historical overview, will be issued during 1992. The international comparative material and the results of the national survey, after being submitted to the second national conference organised by the JEP, will also be published.

Contributors

The editors

DAVID EVERATT is the deputy director of the Community Agency for Social Enquiry, and is national research co-ordinator for the National Youth Development Programme. He has a double first class honours degree from the University of East Anglia and was awarded a DPhil by the University of Oxford for a thesis entitled *The Politics of Non-racialism: White Opposition to Apartheid, 1945-1961.*

ELINOR SISULU is a well-known researcher and writer on African affairs, formerly based in Zimbabwe. She has travelled widely in Africa, and is co-author of a recent study of women in Zimbabwe.

The authors

COLIN BUNDY is Professor of History at the University of the Western Cape, and has published widely on both historical and sociological affairs in South Africa. His publications include *The Rise and Fall of the South African Peasantry*, and (with William Beinart) *Hidden Struggles in Rural South Africa.*

KEN HARTSHORNE is one of South Africa's leading educationists, and has been involved in education since 1938. He taught for many years, then became a schools inspector and finally moved to the planning section of the Department of Bantu Education before leaving the department in 1977. From 1978 onwards he has been associated with a wide range of education projects and programmes in the general field of 'alternative education' as a consultant, adviser and trustee.

Dr Hartshorne holds a BA (Hons) degree in history from the University of London, teaching diplomas in both primary and secondary education, and an MEd (cum laude) from the University of South Africa. In 1975 he was honoured with the award of an honorary LLD by the University of the Witwatersrand, and in 1986 an honorary DLitt by the University of Natal.

STEVE MOKWENA matriculated in 1986 at the Witwatersrand Council of Churches Tuition Project and graduated with a BA (Hons) in history at the University of the Witwatersrand. He worked at the Project for the Study of Violence as a research intern where he researched youth and violence in South Africa. He has also written on violence and aspects of township youth culture.
    Steve Mokwena is currently employed by the Joint Enrichment Project as a youth networker.

MAMPHELA RAMPHELE is deputy vice-chancellor of the University of Cape Town, a medical doctor, and co-author of *Uprooting Povery. The South African Challenge*, which won the prestigious Noma Award for Publishing in Africa.

RORY RIORDAN is the director of the Human Rights Trust in Port Elizabeth. He is editor of the *Monitor* magazine, a director of a number of charitable trusts in Port Elizabeth and writes a political column for the *Eastern Province Herald*.

Introduction

Colin Bundy

If it is true that a people's wealth is its children, then South Africa is bitterly, tragically poor. If it is true that a nation's future is its children, we have no future, and deserve none... (We) are a nation at war with its future... For we have turned our children into a generation of fighters, battle-hardened soldiers who will never know the carefree joy of childhood. What we are witnessing is the growth of a generation which has the courage to reject the cowardice of its parents... There is a dark, terrible beauty in that courage. It is also a source of great pride – pride that we, who have lived under apartheid, can produce children who refuse to do so. But it is also a source of great shame...that (this) is our heritage to our children: the knowledge of how to die, and how to kill.
– Percy Qoboza, *City Press,* 20 April 1986

These are dreadful words. They were written at a dreadful time, at the height of repression during the state of emergency. We have grounds for hope now that were not available then. It is easier to think in the future tense now than it was then. But South Africans cannot, must not, ignore the realities of brutalisation amongst our youth; nor should they overlook the grave social and structural pressures that threaten to deepen and aggravate the alienation and marginalisation of huge numbers of young people in the years ahead. Above all, it is important to understand the urgency, magnitude and complexity of the problems so that they can be addressed.

Certain 'given' or structural factors can be readily identified. The first is demographic. South Africa is in a phase of accelerated population growth, with an annual increase of about 2,6% a year (which means that the total doubles every 30 years).

Population statistics and projections

1951	12 671 000
1960	15 841 000
1985	33 621 000
1990	37 532 000
1995	45 000 000
2000	52 000 000
2020	80 000 000

It is not only the size of the population but its shape that is significant. The demographic profile is typical of a period of rapid growth in that a very large proportion of the population is under the age of 21. More than half of the African population is under the age of 19. In the year 2000, fully 60% of the African population will be under the age of 20.

Political considerations aside, these figures guarantee an enormous pressure on educational resources for the foreseeable future. They ensure the persistence of the direction taken by youth culture. Under any government, the likelihood is that schools will continue to be laboratories and strongholds of protest.

The second and equally obvious structural pressure on the youth is economic. In the 1970s, South Africa entered a period of economic recession. In the 1980s, crucially, South African capitalism did not share in the recovery evinced by most industrialised and newly industrialising economies. The all too familiar symptoms of slowed growth, falling investment, rising unemployment and chronic inflation persisted. They were compounded by an international credit squeeze, balance of payments and exchange rate pressures.

Annual growth rate of GDP

1960-69	average increase of 5,8% p.a.
1970-79	average increase of 3,1% p.a.
1980-89	average increase of 1,3% p.a.

The economic index with the most direct implication for youth marginalisation is unemployment. South African unemployment statistics are notoriously imprecise. Rory Riordan (chapter 4 below) provides a valuable guide to the causes and character of unemployment in South Africa, and its comparability with the phenomenon world-wide. He reminds us that formal unemployment, as a percentage of the economically active population, soared from 22% in 1970 to 40% in 1989. The figure now stands at above 40%.

While the total of out-work expands, the number of available jobs shrinks. Government statistics confirm that between 1984 and 1987 there was a *fall* of 200 000 jobs in mining, construction, manufacturing, electricity, transport and postal services. In the city of Durban, the labour force contracted by 20% between 1982 and 1984. In October 1991 the Development Bank of South Africa (DBSA) announced staggering figures: over the past five years, only 8,4% of nearly 400 000 people entering the job market found employment. (The corresponding figure in the early 1960s was 89%, and 49% in early 1970s.)

The majority of these new job-seekers are of course school leavers. Unemployment is by any standards a mass phenomenon in South Africa, but is visited with particular ferocity on the age bracket 16 to 30 years. In Riordan's case study of Port Elizabeth, over half the total of unemployed are aged 29 or below.

A third structural aspect is urbanisation. The demographic and economic features sketched above will be increasingly concentrated in South African cities. Levels of poverty in rural areas plus the collapse of influx control make pell-mell urban unemployment growth inevitable. People will pour into cities even while unemployment rises and resources shrink. The demands created by this process for housing, health care, schooling, food and employment will be intense.

Much of the new urbanisation will take the shape of 'informal settlement' or squatting. Already an estimated seven million people live in squatter communities in South Africa. A very high proportion of the new urban population will be youthful; and the number of gangs and street children will reach new levels. Steve Mokwena (chapter 2 below) provides case studies that reveal how easily young people are absorbed into crime and violence. A central fact about rapid urbanisation is that it will no longer be possible, as it was under the height of apartheid, to marginalise unemployed youth geographically by exporting them to the bantustans.

Mokwena's chapter opens with the reminder that South Africa is one of the most violent places in the world. A culture of violence permeates the society – not merely in the overt political violence reported in the world's media, but also in spiralling levels of crime (especially rape – the highest known incidence in the world), road and work accidents, and domestic violence. The historical context of colonial conquest, segregation and apartheid is also violent. State policy has for decades involved the large-scale and systematic destruction of family life. Mamphela Ramphele (chapter 1 below) details how particular aspects of apartheid promoted social disintegration in black communities.

In the 1980s, violence became more visible and intense, with mass-based political protest and savage state repression. Young people played a central role in the waves of resistance that ebbed and flowed after 1976. Between 1984 and 1986, 300 children were killed, 1 000 wounded, 11 000 detained, 18 000 arrested on protest charges, and 173 000 were awaiting trial. These figures represent the tip of an iceberg. It is impossible to compute how many hundreds of thousands of children were directly affected through the death, exile, detention or maiming of friends and family members.

Political violence is not the only, nor even the most costly, form of violence. Between October 1989 and February 1991, when 3 200 people died in 'unrest' killings, 26 300 recorded murders took place. The common factor between political violence and other forms of urban violence is that black youths between 15 and 24 years of age were the most frequent perpetrators and victims of violence.

The level of socialised or learned violence amongst young people has intensified in recent years, with devastating consequences. Saths Cooper noted that there was 'very little normality' in the lives of politicised children. There was, he added, 'a very short gap between being the victim of brutality and beginning to commit it oneself.'

Even very young children internalised violence. Games played by toddlers involved Casspirs, AK 47s, ambushes and funerals. A political activist in his early 20s recounted his shock:

> *The four or five year-olds playing on the streets of Soweto played games involving the struggle, singing about Mandela, about Tambo, chanting slogans... I would ask them – these very young fellows – what is the struggle? They would say, 'The struggle ke ntwa! The struggle is fighting!'*

Frank Chikane wrote in 1986:

> *Life in the townships seems to have changed irrevocably.*
> *A township resident said, 'When my two-year old daughter*
> *sees a military vehicle passing, she looks for a stone.'*
> *They too have learned the language of siyayinyova (we*
> *will destroy).*

The spark which ignited so much political violence of the 1970s and 1980s was a mass revolt against bantu education. This gave rise to a cycle of violence in which schools became battlegrounds. Huge numbers of children dropped out of schools, either on organised boycotts or in sheer frustration. Ken Hartshorne (chapter 3 below) finds that 'schooling has both hastened the disintegration of the social fabric, and has itself, in turn...rapidly disintegrated.' It is folly to imagine that the long-term damage done by bantu education can be easily mended, or that the explosive crisis in education can be resolved by a simple return to school.

The inability of teachers and parents to protect the children against the state and grapple in any meaningful way with the massive problems among youth and school children exacerbated and deepened the explosive crisis which cannot now be resolved through a return to school.

These aspects – educational, political, economic, social, demographic and psychological – were only some of the facets of 'marginalised youth' discussed at an important conference, organised by the Joint Enrichment Project, at Broederstroom in June 1991. The conference was important in focusing attention on the problems of black youth; it was attended by delegates from numerous youth organisations (including Azanian National Youth Unity (Azanyu), the Inkatha Youth Brigade, and the ANC Youth League); and it drew up a programme for future research and action.

As working definitions, the conference agreed that 'marginalised youth' referred to people between the ages of about 13 and 30 (including distinct categories of adolescents, post-adolescents and young adults) who were typically neither in school nor in employment, and did not exercise responsibility as heads of households. They are young people who cannot easily be integrated into society's educational, economic, social or political institutions – now or in a future democratic South Africa.

The conference was structured around three major themes: education, employment and work, and the social context. Papers were presented on each of these, and then discussed intensively in commissions and subsequent plenary sessions. Edited versions of the conference papers by Mokwena, Hartshorne and Riordan form chapters of this book, as does the keynote address delivered by Ramphele.

This address highlighted the complex ways in which 'youth' issues are inextricably related to broader economic, social and political questions. She spoke somberly of 'disintegration' and 'social pathology in black communities'; and identified the deep historical roots of contemporary South Africa's vast disparities. Her analysis was particularly valuable because even as she painted a bleak picture of the present, she resisted defeatism or inaction. Instead, her paper concludes with a challenge to black South Africans to reject the 'victim image' and seek creative and holistic solutions.

Ramphele's account of the historical roots of violence in South Africa is developed in Mokwena's 'Living on the Wrong Side of the Law', a vivid anatomising of violence, crime and marginality. Among topics he illuminates, several stand out: 'the crisis of authority' *within* black communities and the intense inter-generational conflict it has generated; the attractions and alternatives provided by gang life to marginalised youngsters; and the way gender oppression lends an extra dimension in the shape of violence visited upon young black women.

Mokwena offers a 'tentative framework for reconstruction'. Possible policy options include a comprehensive social welfare system; a youth employment programme; attention to the measures which address the causes of crime; and attention to the prison system that has nurtured massive youth marginalisation. These will require much hard work and organisation: 'A truly just and non-violent South Africa is not going to be handed over on a silver plate.'

Hartshorne, too, combines analysis of the crisis with some suggestions as to how it may be combatted. In broad terms, he calls for an approach to education in South Africa that keeps in vision both formal and informal modes – one that does not confuse 'education' with 'schooling'. Valuably, he distinguishes between three main categories of school drop-outs and proposes possible responses to the needs of each.

Riordan's tour of 'marginalised youth and unemployment' begins with the observation that unemployment is a worldwide phenomenon. He locates the South African data within this wider frame, and then shifts his focus to a telling case study of Port Elizabeth. He concludes with a level-headed survey of job creation policies and possibilities – and reminds us of the need for research that accurately identifies the size, location, nature and regional variations of 'marginalised youth'. Any coherent policy adopted by any post-apartheid government will depend upon such data.

In addition a post-apartheid government, when it is elected, will be seeking votes from very large numbers of people that the JEP conference regarded as part of 'youth'. It will have to grapple with an educational system that currently adds 300 000 school drop-outs a year to a total of over five million non-literate adults. It will have to distribute resources more equitably even when those resources are cruelly limited. It will have to repair grievous damage to basic social institutions – families, schools, communities. It will be buffeted by heightened expectations for the future even while it inherits the wanton follies of the past.

This is a daunting prospect. How successfully any post-apartheid government contends with it will depend in large measure on how successfully it recognises and responds to the problems that confront young South Africans on a mass scale. This book attempts to contribute to that recognition and response. Its contributors believe that the problems of marginalised youth must be solved so that South Africa may become a nation at peace with its future.

1

Social Disintegration in the Black Community

Implications for Social Transformation

Mamphela Ramphele

Deprived of their natural guides, children of migrants (and all other poor blacks) grow through an insecure, uncertain childhood to an adult life whose sole preoccupation may be to escape the system. There must be a harvest of aggression, with the weeds of violence growing rank within it. The dreadful society is the community of the careless, of those who, treated like boys behave like boys; of those who, having no responsibilities laid upon them owe none to any man. In that chill climate will there be any place for trust? Any hope for human intercourse at all?[1]
– Anthony Barker, 1970

Social Disintegration in the Black Community

Increasing concern is being expressed about the problem of 'the alienated youth' or 'the lost generation' or 'marginalised youth'. The concern is mainly based on the recognition of the potential of this sector of the South African population to destabilise the country, regardless of the nature of the political settlement achieved. A major limitation of this concern is its failure to locate the problem of the alienated youth in a wider analytical framework, and as a symptom of a deeper malaise, being the rapid downward spiral towards total disintegration of the fabric of the black community.

Elements of social disintegration

Communities undergoing social disintegration have been observed to display some of the following behavioural patterns to a greater or lesser extent:
♦ Family breakdowns, with rising rates of divorce, separation, single-parenthood and teenage pregnancy;
♦ High levels of alcohol and drug abuse;
♦ Low performance in all spheres of life including school and skills training;
♦ High crime rates and endemic violence at all levels of social interaction: family, inter-personal, neighbourhood and wider community;
♦ Despair and acceptance of the victim-image;
♦ Flight of skills and positive role models from the townships into higher income areas.
A similar phenomenon observed amongst blacks in the United States has been characterised by social scientists as the emergence of an underclass. Such characterisation presupposes the presence of dominant mainstream classes which can be used as reference points. There is strong empirical evidence of an underclass in the US which under-performs in all respects in comparison with the American mainstream.

Other examples of this phenomenon are to be found in Ireland and the United Kingdom amongst white working-class people. India also has its own pockets of social disintegration. They seem to be communities bereft of any positive motivation to engage in creative strategies to deal with the challenges of life. The first *Carnegie Report on Poverty in South Africa* indicated that a large proportion of poor whites in the 1930s exhibited similar tendencies.

The phenomenon unfolding in South Africa has key features which distinguishes it from its US counterpart. Firstly, since the community affected comprises the majority of South Africans, it cannot be dismissed as functioning outside the mainstream. On the contrary, it threatens to become the mainstream. The term underclass would thus be inappropriate.

Secondly, it would be wrong to describe the South African social disintegration phenomenon as only a black problem. Although one has to acknowledge it predominantly affects blacks, some of the symptoms characteristic of this phenomenon are also in evidence in the wider South African society. For example, violence perpetrated by the state in the form of the Civil Co-operation Bureau and white right-wing groups shows signs of a warped society. So too do the frightening family massacres reported over the last few years. Widespread corruption within government structures has created a crisis of legitimacy of all authority structures in South Africa and has bred a culture of high-class crime within the public sector. The value system of the total South African community increasingly reflects social pathology. It is thus not a racial phenomenon.

It is also true that the problem is not purely an economic one. Not all poor people end up in circumstances of social disintegration. For example, poor people in Zimbabwe and Mozambique have, until the recent increase in Renamo's destructive actions – supported by the South African government – functioned as coherent communities in spite of their plight. Key factors accounting for different responses seem to be the level and pace of urbanisation, the level of perceived deprivation and a sense of entitlement by those seeing themselves as exploited. The large disparities between the haves and have-nots in South Africa provide added impetus to the emergence of a culture of entitlement. Social disintegration is a behavioural problem which has the potential to take over whole communities.

A number of fundamental questions need to be posed in an attempt to come to grips with this phenomenon. What are the causes of social disintegration in South Africa? Why has it taken so long for this phenomenon to surface given the extent and widespread nature of deliberate impoverishment of the black majority by the white minority? What accounts for the continued success of some individuals and groups within the most affected communities? The key to these questions lies in human resilience and the elaboration of survival strategies.

Causes of social disintegration

The perceived social disintegration in the black community can be traced to a number of causes: historical, major developments in the body politic of South Africa in the recent past, and the impact of liberalisation initiated by State President FW de Klerk's speech of 2 February 1990.

Historical causes

Historical causes can be divided into three main categories: demographic, economic and human developmental.

Demographic influences: The conquest of blacks by whites has left deep scars in the black community. The subordination of a majority by a minority required repressive measures to enforce their alienation from the land of their birth and a right of access to land. The Land Acts of 1913 and 1936, together with the Group Areas Act of 1950, were used as instruments of dispossession and impoverishment of blacks.

The impact of conquest has restricted urbanisation of Africans and artificially distributed their numbers in such a manner that led to overcrowding of areas set aside for them.

Successive South African governments utilised the pass laws, influx control regulations and the coloured labour preference policy to control the movements of Africans and to prevent them from participation in the sharing of urban resources. In addition, there was a deliberate policy of under-provision of social services in African townships to discourage family settlement. Housing backlogs, inadequate school facilities, neglect of infrastructural development such as roads, electrification and general public space management, were all designed to make townships unattractive to potential settlers. The net result was total collapse of this inadequate base once the floodgates were opened by the Abolition of Influx Regulations Act of 1986.

Forced removals detailed in the book, *The Surplus People*, as well as Cosmas Desmond's *The Discarded People*,[2] wreaked havoc on families, communities and whole areas. Homelands became the dumping ground of unwanted African people.

The divide-and-rule strategy, perfected by the British colonial rulers, was utilised to great effect to emphasise ethnic diversity amongst Africans and to generate political conflict amongst them centred on competition for scarce resources. Differential resource allocation to bantustan areas became a powerful tool to enforce desirable behaviour by the respective leaders, and to create animosity between communities which had been living together in relative peace for decades. For example, in the early 1980s in the Tzaneen area, Shangaans were pitted against Sothos over access to Shibulane Hospital which was taken away from missionary control and handed over to the Gazankulu homeland catering for Shangaans. It is thus not surprising that the current violence in South Africa has strong ethnic undertones.

Since 1986, the flow from these dumping grounds has put additional pressure on urban resources. Squatter areas all over South Africa are part of the legacy of misguided social engineering.

We are also reaping the bitter fruits of the Group Areas

Act, which wreaked havoc by 'breaking the spider's web' through the systematic destruction of communities at the altar of apartheid. Don Pinnock described this process with respect to District Six removals as being like a man with a stick breaking spider-webs in a forest. The spider may survive the fall, but he can't survive without his web. When he comes to build it again he finds the anchors gone, the people are all over, and the fabric of generations lost.[3]

With the opening up of political space and opportunities outside the disintegrating townships, more and more blacks with the requisite resources are fleeing from these townships and settling in previously exclusive white areas. They are the professional and skilled people who have hitherto provided positive role models for young people in these townships. Their flight deprives the townships of valuable regenerative resources and leads to a concentration of a deviant and crime-ridden sub-culture, which then takes over whole communities.

Economic influences:

♦ Maldistribution of wealth and income is a major feature of South African social relations and has been adequately documented by Wilson and Ramphele.[4] The perception by blacks that they have been deliberately impoverished by successive South African governments is a matter of serious import in the existing conflict.

♦ High unemployment is affecting mainly those who have been disadvantaged and denied education, training and other essential resources for successful economic performance. It is those who have been kept out of the cities and the poorly educated who are hardest hit. They are therefore also very angry and resentful of those seeming to succeed.

♦ The migrant labour system is the single most iniquitous system that could be visited on a people. Its reckless trading on equity – the shameless exploitation of black human capital – further eroded morale in the black community and finally led to bankruptcy with serious consequences for the whole South African society. The immersion of black workers in filth in the migrant labour compounds and the disruption of family life were key elements of this system. Is it any wonder then that migrant hostel dwellers on the Reef were seen on television, talking with pleasure about their next kill in the violence between themselves and township dwellers? The level of dehumanisation caused by this system is frightening.

Human Developmental influences:

♦ Deliberate anti-education through bantu education to produce nothing more than 'hewers of wood and drawers of water' out of Africans has succeeded beyond the wildest dreams of Dr HF Verwoerd, the architect of apartheid.

The process has now gone full circle with products of this system of education constituting the majority of the teaching core with devastating consequences for the quality of black school leavers. Bantu education has also been a source of political conflict leading to widespread school disruptions.

♦ Underdevelopment of potential amongst black South Africans in particular has been an important part of the strategy for domination of the majority by a minority. Those black South Africans who miraculously survived bantu education were met at best by an indifferent job market, and at worst by a hostile one which sought to keep them in their place.

The private sector and other institutions, such as universities, share the blame for this. The Sullivan Code, adopted by some multi-national corporations, was used by some businesses to employ token blacks, without any attempt to develop their full potential. The frustration bred by such hypocrisy further lowered the self-esteem of those affected.

♦ The legacy of job reservation has particularly serious implications for Africans in the job market. Those whites who often boasted that 'my vel is my graad' (my skin is my degree), have benefitted at the expense of blacks who may have been better qualified: income, pensions, housing subsidies and other benefits are all tied to the job one holds. The declining fortunes of the mining industry are bringing the differentials, spawned by job reservation and the collusion of the mining industry in its enforcement, into sharp relief. Conflict is predictable.

Major developments with significant social impact

The Sharpeville massacre of 1960 marked the end of an era in black politics in which young people were beholden to adult leadership. Black people, including political activists, were paralysed through fear of the repressive Nationalist government. Children lost respect for their frightened parents who offered them no protection against police harassment and other problems of poverty.

The Black Consciousness Movement (BCM) addressed itself to this fear and the loss of self-respect blacks had come to accept as inevitable. It inspired blacks to seize the initiative in defining themselves and their struggle, taking responsibility for their own and their country's destiny, and developing self-reliance and pride in their past and their worth as full citizens of South Africa.

The impact of the BCM was felt mostly amongst the youth and professional sectors of the black population. The Soweto uprising of June 1976 was a direct outcome of the defiance bred by the process of conscientisation by BCM, and the willingness by Soweto school pupils to take the risk of challenging the arrogance of bantu education and its prescription of Afrikaans as a medium of instruction.

Once children were thrust 'onto the frontline', it became difficult to sustain traditional social relations between adults and children, and this had serious implications for family life. Children became used to power and control, and refused to yield to the authority of adults whom they despised – their parents and teachers. Conflict became inevitable.

The politics of 'making South Africa ungovernable', which characterised the post-1983 era, has also contributed to the current conflict and social disintegration.

Mass mobilisation, consumer boycotts, school boycotts with the slogan 'Freedom Now, Education Tomorrow', 'People's Courts' and the setting up of alternative structures, all had embedded in them a strong element of coercion and intimidation of those unwilling to participate. Most of the responsibility for enforcing these campaigns rested on the youth. Young people thus assumed enormous powers, including the power to kill. Conflict between young and old was thus heightened.

There were also positive outcomes from this era. The emergence of a strong civic movement has been an essential part of the pressure for change. The launching of the United Democratic Front and the increasing strength of the trade union movement ushered in an era of greater participation by ordinary people in decision-making processes at a local level.

The 'Total Onslaught' and 'Total Strategy' which characterised PW Botha's presidency legitimated and popularised the use of violence against one's political opponents. The Civil Co-operation Bureau was but a small, though dangerous, part of a massive state-directed campaign of terror against government opponents. Both the hunters and the hunted were brutalised by this reign of terror.

Family murders affecting predominantly Afrikaans-speaking white South Africans made their appearance around 1986 like an epidemic. Male heads of households were the murderers of their families, often crowning the sad saga with their own suicides. Something had gone terribly wrong with the fabric of society.

The reform era of 1986 failed to take off. It offered too little too late. PW Botha's refusal to cross the Rubicon killed it off.

Political competition amongst blacks intensified in the 1980s with vigilantes, warlords, comrades and 'com--tsotsis' all fighting for control of the political terrain. Vigilantes were aided and abetted by the security forces, as demonstrated in the case of the KTC squatter camp in 1986. Tension between the youth and adults was exploited to the full and so-called 'fathers' were encouraged to rise

up against the intimidation politics of the comrades. Com-
tsotsis arose out of the legitimation of criminal activities
within black communities in the name of the struggle –
hijacking of private cars, looting of shops, etc.

Warlords are a phenomenon of the Natal region where
chiefs, headmen and squatter leaders loyal to Inkatha
have assumed the role of waging war against the comrades. Thousands of lives and an enormous amount of
property have been lost in the process, while whole communities in rural and peri-urban Natal have been desta-
bilised.[5]

FW de Klerk's 2 February 1990 speech marked the end
of an era and the opening up of new political space, but
economic and social space remains constrained.

Social transition and political upheaval

Escalating political conflict places increasing strain on social relationships – between parent and child, different
generations, different political groups and different interest
groups. The violent nature of this conflict further entren-
ches violence as a means of settling disputes. There is an
ongoing power struggle in the black community as the
stakes for political control increase.

Some of the violence is directed at institutions for a
variety of reasons. Firstly, local government structures and
officials came under heavy attack in the mid-1980s: they
were seen as illegitimate and having failed to address the
real needs of townships residents. Secondly, local mer-
chants were sometimes attacked because they were seen
as exploiters of 'the people' or had refused to contribute to
'the struggle'. Thirdly, the schools and teachers became
targets of anger. The inadequacy of school facilities and
the limitations of unqualified teachers, who were also
found wanting in terms of commitment to 'the struggle',
were cited as reasons for such attacks.

'The family' as a concept also came under severe
strain. Weakened by poverty, overcrowding, migrant labour
and the general sense of worthlessness experienced by

some adults, the family is not adequately poised to cope with politicised and rebellious youths. This resulted in the intensification of tension between the generations, violence within families, and attacks on authority structures at home and school. A void was thus left in the lives of young people.

Right-wing violence is also a feature of the transitional phase we are in. This form of violence is born out of fear of the unknown, and uncertainty about the future for whites in a situation where they no longer have total control of government. There is also anger at loss of privileges which have come to be viewed as rights, including the right to exclude others from sharing resources, the right to treat others as non-beings, and the right to state patronage.

Violence is damaging the very sources of current and potential strength required for the transition.

Black survival strategies

Blacks have not been hapless victims of the historical forces outlined above, but have developed survival strategies. An examination of such strategies and the implications they have for the process of transformation is important.

The economy of affection involves solidarity action with extended family members, peers, homeboys, comrades, political and other groups. This 'economy of affection' has effectively subsidised the main economy by providing social welfare for the indigent and care for the aged, sick and orphaned. Enormous sacrifices are made by those income-earning members of these solidarity groups who have to cope with large dependency ratios. This leads to a denial and delegitimation of the importance of the individual. The development of the individual's full capacity and freedom of choice is compromised in favour of the survival of the group.

Tradition is used as a resource to maintain a semblance of self-respect in the face of the humiliation of conquest and daily exploitation. Selective conservatism is employed by the dominant group – older men – to maintain some level of order and social control. Tradition also legitimates the 'economy of affection' as the 'African way of life'.

Shrinking to fit constrained space – physically, psychologically, politically, economically and intellectually – is also at play. A deliberate process of lowering expectations of the self and others is instituted and legitimated to protect against failure and disappointment. Self-esteem and respect for human dignity of fellow community members is compromised, because those treated like 'boys' end up behaving like 'boys'.

Vacillation between resistance and acquiescence by both individual actors and the group as a whole occurs. The perception of risks attached to resistance ensures acquiescence, but the humiliation of the resultant impotence leads to vacillation.

Short-term gains are maximised at the expense of long-term prospects. Ends and means become confused – crime as a means of survival may become a way of life, while sale of alcohol as a survival strategy creates more problems of poverty and can lead into the drug world.

Crime is a resource used to balance family and personal budgets. The sale of alcohol, dagga and the emergence of a 'shebeen culture' have become entrenched. The pilfering of organisational resources is part of a survival culture. Stealing is regarded as redistribution. Normal behaviour has been criminalised. The law has fallen into disrepute and fails to have any moral or ethical hold on citizens. The criminalisation of family life and the right to seek employment, which occurred under the pass laws, has diminished respect for laws amongst those disadvantaged by such policies. This lack of respect for the law is compounded by the lack of legitimacy of the minority government which enacted such laws.

An image of 'the victim' has developed and is used as a resource for survival within the family, in local areas, nationally and internationally (for example, the 'Victims of

Apartheid Fund' of the European Economic Community). This creates and exacerbates a culture of entitlement amongst those seeing themselves as victims.

The psychology of the victim-image has been elaborated by Steele, an African-American, who is concerned about the position of blacks in America.[6] Blacks are seen as social victims of racist policies which have deliberately impoverished them and diminished their human potential. They are thus entitled as a group to redress. Individual entitlements are more problematic. How is one to balance the infinite demands that would be made on finite resources under such circumstances? How does one choose between the entitlement claims of one individual victim over another?

Individual entitlement also demoralises those on the receiving end. They begin to see society as the agent of change, rather than themselves. For example, black students are victims of wanton neglectful educational policies of the Nationalist government, but they have to apply themselves individually to their studies and utilise whatever support programmes are put at their disposal to succeed. It would be futile to plead victimisation and demand special treatment, unless this is matched by a determination by the individual to take responsibility for his or her own success.

The international community has played an important role in bringing the South African government to the negotiating table, but in some cases individuals and institutions have encouraged the victim role of black South Africans. An industry has emerged in some parts of the world which depends on the perpetuation of the victim-image of blacks for its survival. This international 'South Africa industry' may reinforce the culture of entitlement. If this occurs, it will create problems for a future democratically elected government.

These strategies have ensured the survival of the black community against many odds. Some people have even managed to move beyond survival and are living meaningful lives in spite of their abysmal social backgrounds.

There are thus protective factors which enable certain people to survive and achieve. These have not been properly documented, but include stable family circumstances, where there are high expectations for all to achieve; the presence of positive societal role models; a stable environment (hence the relatively better performance of school children in well-developed rural areas compared to those in the townships); and the presence of an interested adult acting as a mentor to protect against social pathology.

But the failure to service the resource base provided by survival strategies has undermined the very fabric of most black communities. Family coherence is threatened from all directions. Economic hardship and huge dependency ratios have forced parents to choose between employment for survival and attending to their children's emotional and intellectual needs. The choice in favour of survival has further undermined the environment in which black children have to develop.

There has been a 'theft of hope', as Monica Wilson once said of people in rural areas. Despair is widespread. People are being compelled to utilise the least creative survival strategies such as crime (repossession or redistribution) and abuse of alcohol and drugs to dull the pain of humiliation and hopelessness.

The cost of survival strategies

The economy of affection has been found to bear the seeds of nepotism, corruption and high-class crime in other similar circumstances in Africa and Asia. This undermines the emergence of public accountability.

Conformism and collective consciousness result from demands for solidarity action which is essential for survival under difficult conditions. The siege mentality which sometimes results in such circumstances stifles individuality and creativity by delegitimating self-criticism and differences of opinion.

Inferiority complex formation results from being degraded by fellow human beings in most walks of life. This leads to mediocrity, aggressive denial and intolerance of criticism. In the late 1960s the Black Consciousness Movement recognised inferiority complex formation as being one of the greatest constraints on blacks functioning as active agents of history.

Criminality, however legitimated, runs the risk of becoming a way of life. Some shebeens are known to have graduated from sale of alcohol to drugs and sex, with serious consequences.

Tradition can also become a stumbling block to progress because of its use as a resource by powerful groups to entrench their interests. This has particular relevance to the AIDS threat. The use of tradition to legitimate sexism and irresponsible sexual behaviour by men has serious consequences.

Victim-image and its use as a resource to legitimate irresponsibility and the culture of entitlement poses a serious problem for the future. It may be difficult to wean people from the negative attitudes flowing from such a culture of entitlement.

There are also important constraints placed on victims in a situation of widened political space. The values and attitudes required for responsible action in a free society are precisely the ones not rewarded under oppressive conditions. Individual initiative and responsibility for one's own behaviour is discouraged by the demands for solidarity action. Self-interested hard work, as required for studying, conflicts with the desire for immediate gratification offered by a party with friends or attending a meeting which drags on late into the night.

Excellence is understandably considered as a white value in South Africa. The denial of opportunities for blacks to excel in the past has put the very concept of excellence into disrepute. It is thus not surprising that black students have come to aim at 'madoda score' (50%), as long as they pass their courses. Pressure is also sometimes applied to those excelling, because they seem 'out of line'. These attitudes lead some students to conceal their test and examination results to avoid censure. Mediocrity is thus legitimated and entrenched.

The articulation of white guilt and black entitlement which is evident in some institutions in South Africa poses a threat to future social relations. It further disadvantages blacks by treating them as sub-humans or brain damaged creatures, to whom the application of lower standards is justifiable.

All of the above processes undermine the evolution of a democratic culture, and limit the capacity of blacks to act as creative agents of transformation.

Liberalisation and social disintegration

The opening up of political space is a key factor in the social disintegration of the black community. A major reason for the acceleration of this process of disintegration involves the mismatch between political liberalisation, with inevitable rising expectations, and continuing constraints on socio-economic development.

Rising expectations accompanying liberalisation are inevitable and have not been adequately addressed by the government. Bottled-up frustrations and anger are being unleashed. For example, a month after Mandela's release a woman from Khayelitsha squatter area asked the following in letter to the editor of the *Cape Times*: 'Mandela has been released for a whole month now, where is my house?' The same applies in other spheres of life where needs are strongly felt: jobs, schools, health care, etc.

Rapid urbanisation, a consequence of the relaxation of the artificial barriers maintained over many decades, is putting enormous pressure on the limited infrastructure in the townships. Poor and inadequate housing, deteriorating public services and the shrinking job market are adding fuel to the fire of social disintegration.

Increased population movement is accelerating at two levels. Firstly, the flight of positive role models into better and safer areas is increasing, with serious long-term implications for the townships. Archbishop Tutu, an exception to this trend, is on record as saying that he has decided to retain a house in Soweto with the hope of retiring there, in order to continue being a model of hope for those trapped in the townships. Secondly, as the economy worsens, more people are flocking to the urban areas from impoverished rural areas, in search of better prospects.

The liberalisation process reduces respect for institutions. The process is itself an admission that something is wrong in the institutional framework of the society, thus increasing the vulnerability of all social institutions to pressure from disruptive elements. Anti-social and anti-authority behaviour finds easy legitimation and can easily become a way of life.

The miracles of South Africa

South Africans should resist the temptation of total despair and self-pity in the face of the current violence and social disintegration. Given the systematic fomenting of social cleavages and their entrenchment in both law and practice over the past decades, there is a need to celebrate the resilience of black people and the fact that there is still so much goodwill and hope for a better future.

In spite of the legacy of the past and all the traumas of the present, there are still individuals and communities functioning reasonably well, according to all social indicators. For example, professionals, well-functioning families and successful individuals are a significant feature of the black community.

Phola Park, a squatter camp on the East Rand, was until a recent outbreak of violence an example of a well-functioning community in a situation of great deprivation.

Social disintegration will not disappear with the institution of a democratically elected government, as some would like us to believe. On the contrary, a democratically elected government will have greater difficulties dealing with lawlessness, criminality and irresponsibility, because it has to be more responsive to popular demands and criticism.

The implications of all the above will affect all South Africans. The wave of crime and violence is already sapping morale and will continue to erode confidence in the future.

Freedom alone will not bring equality. Equality will have to be achieved through creative equal opportunity programmes with an affirmative action element at all levels of society.

Social disintegration in the black community poses a threat to all South Africans. It is a problem which requires an investment in time and resources, if we are to avoid a downward spiral. There may well be a point of no return in the escalating violence, which will engulf whole communities, as is already the case in some areas of Natal and the Reef.

Pressure arising from those caught in the spiral of disintegration can threaten major institutions of our society. For example, the erosion of the culture of learning has reached worrying proportions. The whole foundation of schooling is under threat.

Experience in the United States indicates that such disintegration is an exceedingly difficult phenomenon to turn around. Throwing money at the problem, as has happened in the US, is not an appropriate solution. Those most affected by disintegration need to have control over any developmental process if it is to have the desired impact.

There are thus a number of challenges we need to face to negotiate the transition in South Africa with any success. We have to acknowledge and name the problems we face: an appalling legacy of deprivation and dispossession, black victim-image and white guilt. We have to resist demands of the culture of entitlement and the use of double standards. We have to establish and enhance commonality in basic human values. Differences where they do occur can only enrich the common ground so established. Finally, we have to insist on essential characteristics of successful institutions: structure, standards, pride and discipline.

An important starting point is to recognise the residual

capacity within the black community to respond to positive intervention. This capacity resides in individuals, support groups and organised pressure groups. There are also safety nets which people have developed over the years which can benefit from being strengthened. The following leverage points can be utilised in transformation and the restoration of hope:

♦ Families to effect different attitudes to child-parent relationships. Parents have to be enabled to deal with rebellion from children, without resorting to violence and rejection;

♦ Churches;

♦ Civics;

♦ Women's organisations;

♦ Youth groups across the spectrum;

♦ Professional organisations;

♦ Support networks – stokvels, burial societies, neighbourhood groups, etc.

Strategies have to be both short-term and long-term and there has to be congruence between ends and means to ensure successful outcomes. We all have to learn new habits of mind in our social interaction.

A conscious effort to invest in the black community has the potential of good returns which will strengthen the above groups and their impact on their communities. The said investments should be seen as part of a conscious effort to part with the past. Development of people should be the goal of such investments and would have to involve a holistic process. The targeting of symbolically meaningful intervention strategies with a potential for a multiplier effect would go a long way to restoring hope and trust.

Notes

1. A Barker, 'Community of the Careless', *South African Outlook*, April 1970.
2. L Platzky and C Walker, *The Surplus People*, Johannesburg, 1985; C Desmond, *The Discarded People. An Account of African Resettlement in South Africa*, Harmondsworth, 1971.
3. D Pinnock, 'Breaking the web: Economic consequences of the

distribution of extended families by Group Areas relocation in Cape Town', Carnegie Conference Paper no. 258, Saldru, University of Cape Town, 1983
4. F Wilson and M Ramphele, *Uprooting Poverty: The South African Challenge*, Cape Town, 1989.
5. Brian Pottinger of the *Sunday Times* estimates that 60 000 people have been displaced in the conflict since the mid- 1980s, as 'combatants carve their territory tree-line by tree-line, stream by stream, path by path' (*Sunday Times*, 9 June 1991).
6. S Steele, *The Content of our Character: A New Vision of Race in America*, New York, 1990.

2

Living on the Wrong Side of the Law

Marginalisation, Youth and Violence

Steve Mokwena

South Africa has the infamous status of being one of the most violent societies in the world. A conservative estimate suggests that over 3 000 people died in political violence across the country in 1990 alone.[1] According to the Human Sciences Research Council's estimates, serious assaults were committed every four minutes, car theft every nine; a break-in every three; a rape every 26 and a murder every 45 minutes in South Africa in 1990.[2] In Soweto alone on a 'normal' weekend, especially at the end of the month, an average of nine murders, 19 rapes and 43 robberies take place.[3]

Black youths feature prominently as both the perpetra-

tors and victims of the violence, both political and criminal.[4] Politicians, preachers and teachers alike have come
to speak of a 'lost generation', hovering in social limbo
with nothing but potent aggression which fuels a life of
crime and violence.

The black youth has been described as a

> group of people already earmarked for failure... (T)hey
> are uneducated, jobless, without saleable skills or social
> credentials to gain access to mainstream life. They are
> rendered obsolete before they can even begin to pursue a
> meaningful role in society.[5]

Why do the black youth feature so centrally in the
violence? What are the forces which have rendered them
'obsolete' and thrown them onto the wrong side of the
law? In an attempt to answer these questions, this chapter
explores
♦ The historical factors which have contributed to the
present status of black youth in our communities;
♦ youth marginalisation in the 1990s;
♦ manifestations of marginalisation in the black communities, focusing specifically on the resurgence of street
gangs and the victimisation of women;
♦ a tentative framework for solutions to the problems of
youth marginalisation and violence.

The legacy of apartheid

Apartheid as a social system has underpinned the process
of marginalisation of black youth, creating perpetual economic dependence and political subjugation. Through a
host of legislative mechanisms, including the Land Acts,
job reservation, influx control mechanisms and apartheid
education, black people were structurally disadvantaged
and thus forced to occupy the bottom rung of the economic ladder. Informal forms of income generation were
criminalised, denying black communities avenues of attaining economic viability. Black youth have been nurtured in

this context of structurally induced poverty.

The Verwoerdian system of bantu education systematically undermined the stability of black youth. Apartheid education denied black youth the necessary tools to enter and participate fully in society. It has also been the site of much trauma, strife, violence and politicisation for black pupils.

Since the 1970s, children have confronted the military might of the Nationalist government on countless occasions to fight for their educational rights. In the process, many have lost their lives.

For those who were steeped in this violent culture, both inside and outside the classroom, the damage is immeasurable. From within the very education system which was supposed to nurture growth and development, black youth have experienced levels of violence incomprehensible to their peers in white schools and in other countries. Many of the same youth have now left school and lie idle with no real prospects for the future.

Marginalisation

While the historical perspective provides a vital backdrop to this analysis, it does not adequately explain the process of marginalisation or the escalation of the phenomenon to the massive proportions of the 1990s. The changing demographic, economic, educational and political status of black youth is of cardinal importance in explaining the social dilemma facing them – and the rest of society – today.

Demographics

The age distribution of the African population has taken on an increasingly 'pyramidal' shape, with the proportion of younger people constantly growing in relation to older people. It is presently estimated that almost 60% of the black population is below the age of 19.[6] The astronomical growth in the size of the youth population has put the youth at the centre of the crisis of social reproduction.

This massive population growth has had several consequences.

Education: Surveys compiled by the South African Institute of Race Relations (SAIRR) confirm that whilst the number of people who enrol for matric examinations is increasing every year, the number of those who manage to obtain matriculation exemptions is steadily declining.

In 1986, 96 000 candidates sat for their examinations. Of these, 50,2% managed to pass with only 16% obtaining matriculation exemption and 37,7% school leaving certificates.[7] In 1988, 169 412 candidates wrote examinations: of the 57,9% who passed, only 16% achieved matriculation exemptions, with 41,4% obtaining school leaving certificates.[8] Out of 177 076 1989 candidates, only 41,1% passed. A tiny 9,7% acquired matriculation exemptions while 31,4% received school leaving certificates.[9] The matric results of 1990 point to a deepening of the crisis. Of the 251 411 candidates who sat for their matric examinations, only 36% passed. The corresponding figure for 1991 was 39%.

While more students enter the system every year, only a small proportion is able to qualify and go either into tertiary education or seek employment. The overwhelming majority is relegated to join the ranks of a growing marginalised youth population. Education has been unable to provide clear connections between schooling and the job world, and has remained ineffective in enhancing the social advancement of youth.

Youth and unemployment: Throughout the 1980s, the number of people churned out into the labour market grew substantially. But this coincided with stagnation of employment opportunities. Recent statistics show that at the present economic growth rate, 50% of the present workforce could be unemployed by the turn of the century. Only 20% of new job seekers are able get employment, compared to 72% in the 1970s. The youth, who constitute an overwhelming majority of new job seekers, are the main victims of unemployment.[10] Some of the effects of unemployment amongst young people can be demonstrated in the following case studies:

> *Gavin Sello, 25 years old, was a matric student in 1986. He did not write his exams in 1986. The following year he went to school and failed his matric because of the sporadic disruption of classes. He made a third attempt in 1988 but gave up. He has been without work since the day he left school. He hopes that one day he will meet someone who will offer him a job. If not, he confesses the only remaining avenue is crime.*[11]

> *Joseph Dlamini, 25, left school in Standard Nine at the age of 21. He now makes a living from selling car parts he steals. He makes enough to afford a fairly comfortable lifestyle. He is quick to point out that no employer will ever pay him the money he is making at the moment. He feels he will remain in the business for another ten years at which point he might have made enough to operate a legal business of his own. He notes that 'things may be changing (politically), but if you were nowhere in the past, you will be nowhere in the future. If I am not educated, where will I fit in?*[12]

It is to 'the world beyond the schoolyard' that this chapter now turns, focusing in particular on the violent path of the 'politically rightless'.

Politics and the crisis of authority in black communities

The genesis of youth-based political resistance in the mid-1970s heralded a new era in South African politics and had a profound impact on various aspects of community life in townships. Both school and home life were directly affected by the growing body of young political activists. The internal dynamics of the student/youth movement for the most part made for a situation where the youth not only directed, but also shaped the political mood of the township.[13] At a social and psychological level, the arrival of the youth on to the political scene dramatically altered the balance of power within the urban communities.

It was during the 1980s, however, that the full impact of the youth's dramatic entry on the political front was felt. The cultural and traditional forces which, to some extent, had held society in place, began to decline noticeably in the face of the resurgent youth movements which swept through the country. The school yard became the terrain of perpetual struggle and this invariably spilled over into the broader community.[14] Acceptable forms of behaviour were challenged directly by the makers of the revolution, the children. Until 1985, Sharf argues, 'inter-generational relationships in African townships, unlike those in other coloured townships, were generally characterised by adults holding authority to lead, discipline and chastise the youth'.[15] Hooliganism or deviance in the communities was thus kept in check. But the ascendancy of the youth in politics undermined adult authority and in some cases challenged it directly.

As an unintended consequence of the political struggle, a potentially chaotic situation began to emerge, as *all* forms of control were challenged. Some argue that it was the strategy of 'ungovernability', preached by sections of the political movement, which is directly responsible for the breakdown of control in the townships.[16]

While the political strategy of 'ungovernability' may indeed be partly responsible for the chaos in black communities, it is certainly not the dominant contributing factor. The strategy of ungovernability was clearly posited alongside that of the attainment of 'people's power'. Street committees, civic associations and other alternative political formations were intended to replace state structures and in so doing, maintain alternative forms of control and discipline in black communities.

The ideals of 'people's power', however, were never able to come to fruition. The state's highly repressive measures were successful in undermining and destroying political organisations and smashing organs of 'people's power', thereby leaving the strategy of 'ungovernability' as the sole weapon in the hands of communities. By clamping down on formal political organisations, the state denied political organisations the opportunity to create a more democratic and consistent political programme.

A major thrust of the state's programme, moreover, was the systematic detention and harassment of the more mature and adult leadership. The political initiatives of the mid-1980s, more than ever before, came to rest on the shoulders of black youth and school children.

As black youngsters took on the challenge of political resistance, they in turn exposed themselves to the apartheid war machine and became key targets of direct state violence. The state did all in its power to demobilise, disorganise and dismantle youth structures.

In this context, it is not surprising that youth resorted to violent tactics. Indeed, violence became the norm of the youth's militant struggle. While white South Africa sang its praises for the 'boys on the border', in the townships black youths chanted slogans of war which glorified the armed cadres of the liberation movement.

Throughout the country the youth were exhorted to become 'young lions' in order to shake off the yoke of their oppression. Black youths became accustomed to the notion of violently engaging in conflict with forces of the state, either in the form of the police and army, surrogates such as vigilantes, or, in the case of Natal, the KwaZulu police. Violence became a socially sanctioned means of attaining change within black urban populations.

The story of Keke Smith is the saga of thousands of other young black South Africans in the 1980s:

Keke Smith describes himself as a soldier, a fully fledged member of Umkhonto weSizwe. As such he presents himself as a person who fought for a political cause in which he claims to have had the support of the people. 'It is for the people that I am serving and it is for the people that I fight. The people support my actions, because these are actions done for the people'.[17]

The impact of youth politicisation on the family

In the process of violent struggle, the youth developed a noticeable arrogance which resulted in intense generational conflict between youth and elders in the community. This is clear, for example, in the experiences of communities in the Western Cape where squatter leaders mobilised against youngsters. In Natal, some political observers have interpreted the war as a struggle between UDF politicised youths and the older, more traditional, Inkatha supporters.

The generational conflict has not always manifested itself in such stark political terms, however, and has taken more subtle and ongoing forms within the privacy of the home. Indeed, the forms of social and political change that were wrought in the 1980s had a very strong impact on the family unit.

The family as the basic organising unit in black communities had been under stress even prior to the beginning of apartheid. Overcrowding, poverty and instability characterised the average black family in the township, placing enormous strain on 'normal' familial relations. Moreover, the practice of migrant labour led to further disruption of families.

The specific contours of politics in the 1980s greatly accelerated the degeneration of family life. Political unrest shook the society at its very foundation and authority in the home, in the street and in the school began to change.

For most of the 1980s political opposition movements provided an alternative learning environment. Where the family was relatively weak and school virtually inoperative, the political culture which was so pervasive in the 1980s acted as a powerful socialising agency. This further eroded the efficacy of the family as a stabilising force.

The failure and the inability of families to minister to the material and emotional needs of youths explains the ease with which youth slide into a life of the streets. It is here that many receive their orientation into a life of violence and crime.

Frustrated expectations: youth and political violence

The 1990s have taken on a new character in terms of youth and politics. The heightened expectations which resulted from the unbanning of the mass-based organisations, the prospects of political transition, and a new sense of latitude in the political arena were a source of zeal for young activists. Yet the slow progress made in the political process, coupled with unrealistic expectations of short-term advances in housing, education and an improved lifestyle, rapidly turned zeal into frustration. These unmet expectations have in themselves become a recipe for violence.

Ironically, the re-entry of the ANC and the PAC into daily political life fed into these frustrations. The new leadership in many respects sidelined the youth from its former position of political prominence in the heady days of a 'people's war' and demanded of them a diplomatic patience radically different from the calls for action in the 1980s.

Despite the new position of youth in the formal realm of the political struggle, they remain central to the political events which have unfolded. Indeed, it is again the youth that have been most affected by the political carnage in the townships and it is they who have become embroiled in violent clashes. Instead of fighting an external enemy (the apartheid government) they are now confronting the 'enemy within' in the guise of rival black parties. It is mainly the youth who are calling for an end to the suspension of the armed struggle so that they can take up arms to protect their communities.

Thabo Segola, 17 years of age. Last week Thabo was a typical schoolboy experimenting with alcohol, bunking classes to sneak dates with his girlfriend and playing soccer in his spare time. Now he stands nervously as a 'soldier' on a township street corner, armed with a golf club and ready to battle Zulu-speaking warriors. He, like many thousands of other youths in Reef townships and Natal, has become engulfed in a virtual civil war with Zulu-speakers living in single sex hostels in the townships.[18]

The onus is on the political organisations across the spectrum to develop programmes which will harness the political energies of the youth, while at the same time laying the foundation for a non-violent democratic political culture which is desperately needed in the reconstruction of a new society.

It is unacceptable to refer to the black youth as a 'lost generation'. This judgmental terminology masks the processes which have alienated black youth from the sources of wealth and power in this society. Colin Bundy points out that

By any stretch of the sociological imagination, the recipe for marginalising and alienating a generational unit is comprehensive enough. Take politically rightless, socially subordinate, economically vulnerable youths; educate them in numbers beyond their parents' wildest dreams, put them in educationally grotesque institutions; ensure that their awareness is shaped by punitive social practices in the world beyond the schoolyard – and then dump them in large numbers on the economic scrap-heap.[19]

Marginalisation, street gangs and violent youth culture

Many of the young people who were the one-time engine of the South African liberation struggle now lie idle and disaffected. They are a potential menace with a capacity to commit indescribable atrocities against their own people. The deepening crisis of marginalisation is feeding directly into the growth of a violent and criminal youth culture manifested particularly in the escalation of youth gang formation in the townships.

The bellicose youth gangs which have multiplied over the past few years are a concrete index of marginalisation.

They are a response to the economic and social constraints facing young blacks.

Contrary to the widespread belief that people join gangs due to laziness or inherent vice, the rise of criminal youth gangs should be seen primarily as a survival technique in a society which has condemned many young blacks to a life of poverty and desperation.

The destabilisation of family life and the collapse of the education system have contributed to the formation of street gangs. Many youngsters, in an attempt to escape their overcrowded and often poor homes, have opted for a life in the street gangs.

Clinton is 14 years old. He was brought to see the social workers by his distressed mother. He is the eldest son and a brother to three sisters. His mother says that he has not been going to school regularly. Although he denies it she swears that he is now part of the Americans (an established gang in the township). The mother feels that she is responsible for what is happening to him, and believes that he is joining the street life because of the conditions at home. She lives in someone's backyard and has no stable source of income.[20]

Gangs also provide possibilities for material advancement in the absence of any possibility of employment. This has resulted in many youth seeking social and economic survival on the wrong side of the law.

The political crisis of the mid-1980s, followed by the successive states of emergency, fundamentally disturbed the social cohesion of the black communities. 'A by-product of resistance was the rise in youth militancy. Disdain for traditional and parental authority added to the collapse of an informal network of control and order. The youth, alienated and angry and left with no role models, eventually drifted into gangs.'[21]

Gangs also arise out of a need to create entertainment and excitement. There is a chronic lack of recreational facilities in the townships. In an attempt to deal with boredom, youths are forced into the street for entertainment. This is where many are tutored into a life of violent crime and gangsterism.

Vast areas within black communities have now been occupied by gangs. For a considerable period, areas of Soweto were dominated by the notorious Jackrollers, Pimville has been occupied by the Amajapan and recently the Three Million gang has unleashed a reign of terror in the Kroonstad township in the Orange Free State.

Gangs provide an alternative home for marginalised youngsters. They are a source of emotional and material support. They are also an attempt by the powerless and the alienated to obtain a sense of power, status and belonging.

Gangs are an embodiment of a viciously violent street youth culture. It is here where violence finds acceptance as a normal way of life. Within this machismo culture, violence is a means of self-assertion and often the only known conflict resolution mechanism. It is within this 'sub-cultural alternative'[22] that crime becomes acceptable as a normal and acceptable way of life. Social deprivation led to the acceptance of crime as a way of life beyond the confines of gang life. Many adults in honest employment also passively accept criminal behaviour as a way of life. In some ways children grow up seeing their parents turning a blind eye to crime or encouraging it by pilfering at work or even buying stolen goods. In gang life and other decidedly criminal formations, organised criminal behaviour is blown into unimaginable proportions. Cars are hijacked in broad daylight. Women are abducted in front of helpless spectators. Known criminals boast about their exploits in public, feeling no shame and making no effort to hide from the law.

Responses to gangs and youth crime

'Standard' responses adopted to deal with gangs and gangsterism do not deal with the root causes of the problem and thus contribute to the forces which eject 'deviant' youth from society.

Community responses range from 'witch hunts' for notorious gang members who are then subjected to 'instant justice', to street patrols over specific periods, or in some cases in-depth campaigns.[23] Social workers in Nicro, Cape Town, have looked into involving the communities, including gang members, in campaigns around the issue of youth gangs and crime in the different communities.[24]

In some cases these community actions have led to fierce and prolonged battles in the townships which take the form of revenge attacks and a spiral of counter attacks. In other cases, gang members have been handed over to the police and forced to stand trial.

The problems posed by gangs are compounded by the legacy of apartheid policing and the breakdown in community trust of existing law enforcement agencies. While police policy is to eradicate such gangsterism (and in some areas specific units have been established for this purpose), allegations of police connivance with and use of gangsterism still abound. The consequence is an inevitable increase in violence as residents resort to 'legal self-help' in an attempt to deal with the problem.[25] Police responses, on the other hand – even if directed at eradicating gangs – fall short of their aim since they too tend to be reactive initiatives dealing with the symptoms rather than the causes of the problem. Furthermore, police gang-busting moves are seldom based on co-operation with the community.

Most community responses are not proactive. In the case of community witch-hunts, the community responds with alarming (albeit understandable) anger once the damage has already been done. A lack of understanding of the problem often means that, in affected townships, the community does not have the organisational framework or perspective to deal with gangs in a proactive way. This suggests a need for a well co-ordinated strategy on the part of township residents to deal with youth criminality.

This response should be accompanied by campaigns and strategies which attempt to deal with the root causes of the problem in both the short and the long term.

Violence and young women in black communities

In addition to contending with socio-economic impediments, black women have to bear the brunt of various forms of direct violence from males in their communities. The increase in youth violence has most noticeably been accompanied by a further increase in violence that is directed against young women.[26]

Marginalisation refers to the systematic disempowerment of people with the resultant inability to develop psychologically, economically and otherwise. As such, women are even more marginalised than young males. In a patriarchal society like South Africa, governments and policy makers often show little sensitivity to the problems facing women in general.

> *When you leave your child alone in the home she is not safe. And in the street, she is not safe. And in the school she is not safe. There is nowhere that she can walk and be safe. Girls are afraid somebody in a car will stop them and say 'get in.' When they walk in the street they are raped by men with guns. Sexual abuse happens so much that some students stop going to school.*[27]

Rape is by no means the only form of violence against women. Young women have to contend with many other forms of sexual harassment on a daily basis. Violence against young women occurs in part within the framework of a male-dominated society. Men have been taught to define their power in terms of their capacity to effect their will, especially over women, with or without the consent of those involved.[28] This is an integral part of a society which prescribes different gender roles, a society where young males are taught to be assertive and masculine, and where women are expected to be subordinate and submissive. It is a context in which young black men grow up seeing their mothers and other women living under the domination of their fathers and adult males.

In South Africa racism compounds this dynamic through the creation of powerlessness and impotence which imposes a form of 'inferiority complex' upon its victims. Black males of all ages have to deal with an inferior status often experienced as emasculation in society and in the workplace, where they are treated as 'boys'. This inferior status contradicts their socialisation and leads to chronic feelings of inferiority. It is accompanied by deteriorating social and economic circumstances which lead to high unemployment. Psychologists have pointed out that, for many men, work is inextricably tied to gender expectations and their experiences of masculinity. Unemployment is thus experienced as a personal, rather than a social, failure. A conjunction of the factors mentioned above creates a situation where violence is used as a means of increasing self-esteem. Women, as less powerful persons, become the victims of displaced aggression and a symbolic reassertion of masculinity and control.

In the past two years the phenomenon of 'jackrolling' has emerged. This refers to the way gangsters cruise the township streets in search of women who are then abducted in broad daylight and whisked away to places where they are gang-raped. For a considerable period, 'jackrollers' terrorised women in many parts of Reef townships with a seeming impunity.

According to Isabella, a 17-year old student in Soweto, 'I am afraid of the Jackrollers. They are affecting all of us as girls. We are not safe any more. We can't even walk in the streets without being harassed by hooligans.[29]

Young women are thus victimised both directly and indirectly. They have to be ultra-cautious about their movement, what they wear and which places they visit. These added restrictions further entrench their sense of inferiority and marginalisation.

Young women are further marginalised by other factors intrinsic to black communities. Unlike young men, they bear the brunt of a cumbersome domestic economy which involves virtual domestic servitude. This reinforces their subservient role as women, and in the long run interferes with their ability to succeed in spheres beyond the domestic arena. Thus, a greater percentage of women fail to acquire tertiary level education than men.

Young women are further disadvantaged by unwanted pregnancies. Teenage pregnancies are part of our index of marginalisation and social breakdown. Little is said about the lack of adequate contraception in black communities, and teachers, parents and preachers often remain opposed to proper sex education.

A framework for reconstruction

The social process that has been referred to as 'marginalisation' refers to the comprehensive disempowerment of black communities, in particular the youth. It is an expression of powerlessness, not only in the context of political rights and institutions, but in society as a whole: economic powerlessness, exclusion from the social welfare system, educational impoverishment and legal exclusion.

To combat marginalisation, reconstruction needs to be comprehensive. In particular, an organisational network must be generated which empowers black communities at every level. This should be built at a local level to minister to the political, economic, legal and welfare needs of these communities.

Social welfare: Changing the context of marginalisation requires initiatives at both the macro and micro levels. Given the size and nature of the problem, there is a need for the development of a comprehensive social welfare programme. This should be aimed at developing disadvantaged communities and providing them with the resources needed for creating conditions in which the marginal status of black youths can be reversed.

Educational reconstruction: The development of a demo-cratically accepted education system is vital. This should provide education which will empower human beings and provide them with the skills necessary to perform effec-tively in society.

Ways must be found to deal with the present backlog in education. A revamped education system needs to cater for the needs of those who have not completed their schooling, especially secondary schooling. Adult education programmes which are geared towards attracting 'marginalised' youths are of key importance. Present adult education schemes are not built to minister to the needs of educationally peripheralised people. An alternative sys-tem must target this specific group and make provision for accessible day-time tuition and other activities. This programme should concentrate on providing job-related skills.

This recommendation is made in the light of the recent announcement by the government proposing free and compulsory education to children of all races for the first seven years of their schooling. It is essential for any fu-ture education system to grapple with the historical back-log of 'apartheid education'. The casualties of apartheid education will remain central in the 'new' political dispen-sation, and cannot be written off as a bad debt.

Employment creation: The social consequences of youth unemployment have clearly pointed to the looming threat of social decay. The development of a comprehensive youth employment programme is vital. Such a programme requires large financial inputs, and policy makers and economists need to explore ways in which young people can be integrated into the labour market.[30]

Such programmes could also be undertaken by busi-nesses, both big and small, as part of their social respon-sibility activities. Providing jobs is by far the most important weapon against marginalisation.[31]

Anti-crime and anti-gang initiatives: Since marginalisa-tion manifests itself in an increase in youth criminality, it is

important to develop a long-term anti-crime programme.[32]
This will require all groups concerned with the increase in
violent crime – service and welfare organisations, civic organisations, political organisations, youth groups across
the social and political spectrum, as well as industrial and
research groups – to work towards effective policies to
combat youth crime. Responses to youth crime must be
informed by a well-researched proactive approach.

Reforming the prison system: South Africa is said to
have one of the world's largest proportionate prison populations. According to the South African Prisons Services
report for the year ending December 1991, there was a
daily average of 96 540 persons in prison.[33] The most
likely candidates for imprisonment are to be found within
the marginalised youth population.

Many marginalised people find themselves on the
wrong side of the law and end up in prison. The question
to consider is whether the correctional services as they
exist serve as a mechanism of reintegration. Does our
present system enable ostracised and alienated people to
function in society, or does it further deepen the crisis?
Research has shown that 72% of those who enter the
prison system are likely to return to its walls. This already
high recidivism rate is even higher amongst people below
the age of 30.

Arthur et al perceive the chief products of the prison
system as being rancour, resentment, degradation and a
widening gulf that separates 'us' and 'them'.[34] This gulf is
further widened by the stigma that goes with imprisonment: ex-prisoners are held up as objects of fear to children and denied work in a society that has neither forgotten
nor forgiven, thus laying waste the individual's perception
of having 'paid his/her debt' to society.

Persons released from prison find themselves confronted with a serious lack of resources which serves further to entrench their unemployability. The present prison
system contributes, in the long term, to marginalisation
and does not serve to rehabilitate offenders. There is
therefore a need to re-evaluate the manner in which

society deals with those who find themselves on the wrong side of the law. The failure to do so means that people will invariably repeat the tragic cycle of committing crimes, being imprisoned, going back to crime after release and finding themselves back in prison.

Many marginalised youth regard the prison as a refuge where, despite the isolation and the violence, one is at least guaranteed shelter and food. Many also regard the process of imprisonment as a way of acquiring education which will equip them for a life in the streets. A prison record is also regarded as a status symbol.[35]

Psychological reconstruction: There is no doubt that the broad political and economic forces which lead to marginalisation have had a tremendously negative psychological impact on young people. Many of those who have experienced and lived with violence are psychologically bruised and have come to accept violence as a way of life and an appropriate means of conflict resolution.

How do we repair the adverse psychological effects of growing up in a violent society? How can the necessary support to transform the psyche of marginalised black youths, and provide the human resources which are desperately needed in order to combat the growing tide of marginalisation, be provided?

Societal transformation must be accompanied by psychological healing. But psychological reconstruction without adequate social reconstruction will not make a significant difference. Social change does not take place in a vacuum. People are required to effect the change. The youth are indeed the people who will have to play a role in changing and building a new society.

The nature of the change is such that people, including the youth, have to demonstrate perseverance and patience. Given the ever-deteriorating conditions, black youth tend to live for the present. Vogelman suggests that

The lack of long-term planning is manifest in a number of areas. It can be seen in the widespread nature of teenage pregnancies, a high level of substance abuse, in particular

alcohol intoxication, a lack of concern about an education or skills and macho violent behaviour which frequently endangers them in terms of arrest.[36]

The youth have been socialised into a political culture of defiance in which all forms of authority have been eroded. It is important to rebuild authority structures which are acceptable to all, especially youth. At the same time, it is important to develop the psychological framework which will make such a transition possible.

As youth drift into the quagmire of material frustration, they threaten to develop into a 'fourth force'[36] which, because of its anarchic, sporadic and unorganised ways, could sabotage the process of building a new society.

Real change will only come about once the entire political and economic system that has led to the marginalisation of black youth is eradicated. This in itself will require a great deal of organisation and hard work from within black communities. A truly just and non-violent South Africa is not going to be handed over on a silver plate.

Notes

1. G Simpson, S Mokwena and L Seal, 'Political Violence in 1990', in M Robertson (ed), *Human Rights and Labour Law Yearbook: 1991',* Cape Town, forthcoming.
2. *Citizen,* 20 November 1990.
3. Statistics compiled by the Project for the Study of Violence. In the first four months of 1991, it was claimed that 115 vehicles (about four a day) were hijacked in Soweto (*Sowetan,* 13 February 1991).
4. According to S Khumalo, regional developer of the National Institute for Crime Prevention and Rehabilitation of Offenders (Soweto branch), the average offender in South Africa is black, between the age of 16 and 26, and often has meagre education.
5. DG Gibson, 'The Black Underclass. Poverty, unemployment and the entrapment of ghetto youth', London, 1980.
6. L Vogelman, 'Black Youth in South Africa', unpublished paper, 1990.
7. South African Institute of Race Relations, *Race Relations Survey, 1988/89,* Johannesburg, 1989.
8. South African Institute of Race Relations, *Race Relations Survey, 1988/89,* Johannesburg, 1989.
9. South African Institute of Race Relations, *Race Relations Survey,*

1989/90, Johannesburg, 1990.
10. See R Riordan, 'Marginalised Youth and Unemployment' (chapter four in this collection) for a fuller discussion of unemployment.
11. Connie Molusi in *Business Day*, 21 August 1990.
12. Connie Molusi in *Business Day*, 21 August 1990.
13. S Johnson (ed), 'The Soldiers of Luthuli', in (ed) S Johnson, *South Africa: No Turning Back* , London, 1988.
14. J Hyslop, 'School Student Movements and State Education Policy', Unpublished paper, 1988.
15. W Sharf, 'The Resurgence of Urban Street Gangs and Community Responses', in (ed) D Hansson and D van Zyl Smit, *Towards Justice. Crime and State Control in South Africa*, Cape Town, 1990
16. Interview with S Maseko, publicity secretary of the Azanian Students Convention, 23 March 1991.
17. G Simpson, 'Report to the Klerksdorp Magistrate's Court in the Matter of *S vs Smith and Mailane*, 27 November 1990.
18. Bryan Pearson, *Natal Witness*, 20 August 1991.
19. C Bundy, 'Street Sociology and Pavement Politics: some aspects of student/youth consciousness during the 1985 school crisis in Greater Cape Town', *Journal of Southern African Studies*, 13(3), April 1987, 313.
20. Interview at Nicro, Cape Town, 14 May 1990.
21. Nicro, *Gangs, 'The Search for Self-Respect'*, Cape Town, 1990.
22. See A Cohen, 'The Delinquent Subculture', in M Wolfgang et al (eds), *The Sociology of Crime and Delinquency*, second edition, 1970; C Glaser, 'Anti-Social Bandits, Cultural Resistance and the Tsotsi Subculture on the Witwatersrand during the 1940s and 1950s', paper no. 278 presented to the African Studies seminar, University of Witwatersrand, September 1990.
23. Interview with Michael Maphongwane, Kayelitsha civic leader, who was subsequently killed in July 1991.
24. Interviews conducted at Nicro, Cape Town, with Lucas Malekane and Hulene Hadje, 14 May 1990.
25. Interview with Captain Ngobeni at Protea police station, May 1991.
26. Adriaan Vlok, at the time Minister of Law and Order, quoted on Radio 702 News, 3 April 1990.
27. Mary Mabaso, unpublished interview by Diana Russell, March 1990.
28. CF Swift, cited in M Motsei, Building Real Support for Battered Women, unpublished paper. Project for the Study of Violence, 1990.
29. Project for the Study of Violence workshops, held in Orlando, Soweto, April 1990.
30. See R Riordan, 'Marginalised Youth and Unemployment' (chapter four in this collection).
31. Glaser, writing about the 1950s, argues that the state managed to deal with what it perceived as the 'Native Juvenile Delinquency Problem a parallel historical dilemma facing the youth in the 1950s

by providing jobs, however menial, on a large scale, and expanding the education system.

32. L Vogelman and G Eagle, 'Overcoming Endemic Violence Against Women', 1990. Seminar paper, Project for the Study of Violence, University of the Witwatersrand, 1990.
33. Parliamentary question: Dave Dalling to Minister of Correctional Services, *Hansard,* 17 February 1992.
34. Cited in Vogelman and Eagle, 'Overcoming Endemic Violence Against Women'.
35. Interview with Mpho Serobe, a youth from Diepkloof,17 April 1991.
36. L Vogelman, 'Black Youth in South Africa. Some Factors to Consider', unpublished paper, 1990.
37. This term was used by Prince Morare at the Soweto Crime Convention, held on 8 May 1991.

Research for this article was undertaken while the author was employed at The Project for the Study of Violence, University of the Witwatersrand.

3

Education
and Employment

Ken Hartshorne

It is absolutely right to place the issue of alienated youth in the context of social and family disintegration. The fabric of society becomes torn when there are imbalances between youth and adults; when acceptable, working relationships between the two break down; when youth 'takes over' and adults abdicate. Education can both contribute to the weaving of a strong societal fabric, and to the repair of breaks in the fabric. But in our society, education (and in particular schooling) has been one of the major factors damaging and weakening the fabric. Schooling has both hastened the disintegration of the social fabric, and has itself, because of this, rapidly disintegrated.

This chapter focuses on the area of education and work. A major indicator of present-day African youth is that they are *unemployed* – both because many are *unemployable* as a result of a lack of basic education skills, and because there are not enough jobs to go round.

Some introductory statements on education are necessary to place the discussion on 'education and work' within a realistic context that will not idealise what education (including schooling and training) is capable of achieving.

There is a confusion between *schooling* and *education*. They are not the same: the former is but part of the latter. When we speak of the education system we are generally referring to the school system. South Africa does not yet have an 'education system' that integrates all the aspects of education – formal, non-formal and informal. Therefore, when we speak of 'education and work' we are dealing with a much wider canvas than schooling alone. What happens to people before they go to school (family upbringing, socio-economic conditions, etc), outside of school (peer groups, environmental influence, etc) and after school (further adult education and training, etc) is at least as important as what happens in school. Attitudes to, knowledge of, and capacity for coping with the work situation are as powerfully influenced by these factors as by the school.

Too much is expected of schooling, particularly in developing 'third world' environments. Schooling systems reflect the society of which they are a part, and are generally used by the state to bolster the political and economic systems in existence. While schooling systems have creative possibilities, they can become active change agents only with state support and initiatives, backed by broad political will and popular acceptance. Schooling systems cannot solve economic problems, provide employment or reduce social and political inequalities. They must be used for those things they are best equipped to do and not be expected to serve as a general rescue net for all the problems of society that others have not been able to do anything about!

Schooling systems should be concerned with the teaching, learning and development of knowledge and its application; values and attitudes; skills – personal, social, civic, work-related and creative; and independent thinking.

Knowledge is not simply the collection and reproduction of facts from a textbook, but the ability to make use of the knowledge, together with its relevance to the 'real life', outside the school.

Values have to do with issues such as democracy or authoritarianism, co-operation or competition, tolerance or violence, what is common or what is different in our society, self-interest or regard for the common good, etc.

Skills can be related to issues like literacy and numeracy, learning to work together with other people, coping with life, how to carry out the responsibilities of a citizen, and issues of work and employment. In the case of the latter skills, it is doubtful whether the school, except perhaps in the very late stages, is the best environment for the learning of specific technical skills.

What is crucial for all work situations is that the school should teach young people to think, to apply their knowledge in order to solve problems, to work well together, to use their own initiative, to develop a 'get-up-and-go' spirit and to be adaptable. These are far more important than the acquisition of a few technical skills.

In carrying out these primary purposes the school is subjected to pressures from a number of conflicting interests, and has to maintain a very delicate balance between the needs (and wants) of the individual learner, the society from which he/she comes, the economy that makes claims on the school, and the state, which has its agenda. Whatever other needs it responds to, the school's first concern has to be for the individuals placed in its care, and what it can do for them as human beings now and in the future. It therefore has to take into account their need to be able to earn a living as one of many needs that people have if they are to live full, satisfying lives. This is not really at issue: the questions rather involve how to achieve the most effective balance, the 'right mix', for schooling to become more relevant to real life needs; how to bring this about; what can properly be expected of the school; and what has to be done by other institutions (social, economic and political).

Education and work

The debate on education and work cannot be contained within a simplistic discussion of 'academic' versus 'technical, vocational or career' education. In many ways this is a false dichotomy. On the one hand, a relevant, effective academic 'education' provides the background of language, mathematics and science that many modern work situations demand. What matters is *how* they are learned and taught, and whether they are capable of being *used* outside of the school.

What is perhaps of most value to any country and to any economy is the provision of sound, basic primary education (literacy, numeracy and basic life-skills) which provides a platform on which further education and training can take place; yet this is often defined as 'academic'!

On the other hand, there is no reason why schooling at the secondary level, for example, that is defined as 'technical' should not also provide a broad educational experience for the learner. Language, mathematics and science are still required, and again what matters is how they are learned and taught, and how relevant they are to the world outside the school.

The crucial issue is that in South Africa, as elsewhere, a false distinction has been made between 'intellectual' and 'manual' work, and this has been reinforced by colour and class differences. While there may be a place for schools with a 'special bias' at the senior secondary level, an over-emphasis on this kind of 'solution' will lead only to a strengthening of the intellectual/manual divide. It is the future national, common curriculum for all schools that is the major challenge. This is not just a matter of 'revising' or 'making more relevant' what is already in the school curriculum, but of considering both what should be jettisoned and what needs to be added in order to bring the school nearer to the society it serves, one part of which is the 'world of work'. Another way of putting this is that throughout the curriculum, there needs to be stronger links between theory and practice.

In the Southern African Development Co-ordination Conference (SADCC) countries surrounding South Africa these broad curriculum issues are being debated under the banner of 'Education with Production'. The proponents of this approach point out that

> *Important and vital elements missing from conventional curricula include a comprehensive knowledge of culture, what it is and how it relates to material life; of technology, its links to science and mathematics, its diversity and complexity; of development and of production, and of the social, cultural, political, economic, financial and material issues that relate to both; of management and all its complex and diverse functions, and its linkages to social stratification; of the historical interrelationship and interaction between human society and the environment; and of the real-world, direct linkages between mathematics and science, and production and development. Here, of course, are the basic areas of knowledge which precisely do link theory and real practice...*

In order to bring these elements into the school, curricula have been prepared in study areas such as cultural studies, environmental and social studies, development studies, and fundamentals of production.

In broad terms, particularly at the secondary level, South African schooling has failed to develop what might be called social, political and economic 'literacy', and the experiences of other countries in this regard are worth studying.

In many developed countries, eg Britain, USA and Germany, the relation between school and work has been approached not by major changes to school curricula, but by providing a 'bridging experience' during which the young adult learner spends part of his/her time in school and the rest in the work situation. This is an alternative approach to the issues of theory and practice, but depends on highly sophisticated support from the private sector and is unlikely to function well where there are high levels of unemployment. Yet it is an approach that might be used on a limited scale in the urban, industrialised sector in South Africa, as one of the many ways used to tackle the problem.

Interest groups

The attitudes and approaches of the various groups that have interests in what happens in the schools are of some importance to the discussion of education and work.

Industry and commerce are right to stress the need for skilled people, but it is their responsibility to produce most of these skills as they are the primary beneficiaries. The general economy may also benefit, but the driving force of the free enterprise system is benefit through profit. What industry and commerce can rightfully expect from the schooling system is that it produces people with a good basic education so that training is possible, effective and financially viable; and that at another, higher, level, it is of such a quality that basics such as language, mathematics and science are effective and relevant to their needs.

While it would be useful for business to specify in more precise terms what 'characteristics those people should have in order to make them employable and trainable' and to have a say in the setting up of new national curricula, there are other interests that have an equal right to a say. If the formal sector was able to produce a larger proportion of new jobs, it would be in a stronger position to make demands. What 'big business' requires of its workers, for example, might be quite different from what is required of those who will have to create their own jobs in the 'informal sector'. There will have to be balances in the new national curricula that will have to be negotiated among conflicting interests.

The trade unions have right on their side when they note that people are not only workers, and that schooling must prepare young people for living as well as working; and that skills should not be so narrowly defined that workers are 'caught in a trap' at a certain level from which it is difficult to advance. The way forward would certainly seem to be joint, co-operative efforts of employers and trade unions in any education and/or training programmes meant for workers or their children. The level, content, approaches and methods of all such programmes should be negotiated and agreed upon, not imposed from the top. There is also room for trade unions themselves to take responsibility for the further education of their members through initiatives of the kind, for example, represented by the WEA (Workers Education Association) in the history of trade unionism in Britain.

However, neither employers nor trade unions, because of their particular interests, are able to articulate the needs of those who are neither in school nor in employment. To some extent, broad community and political organisations have placed this issue on the table, but have done so in very general terms. The educational, training and employment needs of illiterate adults, unorganised workers such as those on white farms, unemployed youth, those in squatter camps and resettlement areas – to name but some of the groups with little power or influence – have received little attention. For the purposes of this article, I now focus on what I regard as the most difficult group to reach, and the most potentially 'explosive' group – youth out of school and unemployed young adults.

Alienated, hard-to-reach, unemployed youth

This major grouping shares both a common history (which has been outlined in other contributions to this volume) and many common characteristics: the great majority are unemployed; most are 'politicised' (but not necessarily with the same 'politics'); most have grown up in a culture of violence and are no strangers to it; and most, in educational terms, have a sense of failure. They have 'dropped out' of the schooling system, rejected it or been rejected by it, failed to meet its requirements, or, having survived all 12 years of it, emerged without anything to show to a certificate-obsessed society and business sector.

However, it is not a monolithic group. Within it there are different needs and situations which require a whole range of strategies and solutions if its members are to be 'rescued' and reintegrated into society. What I now intend to do is to try to give some rough 'size and shape' to the problem, and to break down this major grouping into three main groups, each with two sub-groups.

Particular groups have their own specific problems. For example, about 50% are girls and young women. Do they respond the same way as the men or are they coping in other ways? Very briefly, the three groups are

Group A

1. *Those with no schooling at all. (In 1988, for example, there were about two million youngsters between the ages of seven and 16 who were not in school. However, this does not mean that all of them have had no schooling.)*
2. *Those who dropped out of school before completing Std 4, and who can therefore be regarded as not literate or numerate. (In numbers this is the biggest sub-group: each year one third of a million youngsters are being added to the conservatively estimated five to six million non-literate South Africans.)*

Group B

1. *Those who completed primary schooling but went no further.*
2. *Those who dropped out in secondary school.*

In total this sub-group amounts to 225 000 school leavers per year.

Group C

1. Those who passed senior certificate, but failed to gain matriculation exemption.
2. Those who failed to gain any certificates in the final secondary school leaving examination.

This group is being added to by about 125 000 per year. In the ten years from 1980-1989, 521 370 pupils completed secondary schooling with a matric or senior certificate, but about 515 000 had to leave Std 10 without any formal certificate, having failed the final examination.
I have omitted those with a matriculation certificate from group C, optimistically believing that they have a fighting chance, but in practice many of them require further support and re-training because of the low quality of their results and the absence of science and mathematics.

On the one hand, given the numbers involved and the resources available, it is clear that certain tough priorities will have to be established in allocating resources to 'rescuing' the above groups. It will not be possible to do everything that is required nor to do it all at once. On the other hand, by breaking down the massive problem into broad categories, it becomes possible to establish both priorities and a range of strategies to deal with different parts of the problem. In very general terms my perception of the order of priority would be as follows:
♦ To make the most of the potential resident in the group that has completed secondary schooling, with or without certification (group C).
♦ To give attention to the younger members of group A who have not achieved a platform of basic education on which further education and training can be based.
♦ To provide skills training and 'morale building' for group B. State intervention in terms of 'youth brigades', 'land service', 'civilian conservation corps' and like concepts will probably be necessary. The private sector, including business interests, will have to make a major contribution towards further education and provision of training.

I now turn to a rather more detailed consideration of each of these priorities.

Secondary school leavers without certificates

There is no single approach or strategy. The following are some of the possibilities, nearly all of which will lie outside the scope of formal schooling.

1. Opportunities to repeat senior certificate, and at the same time to upgrade subjects such as mathematics, science and English. There is place here for adult education centres, privately funded programmes, correspondence colleges and distance teaching strategies backed up by local tutorial groups.
2. Opportunities to move away from the so-called 'academic' background already gained in the secondary school to technical and commercial skills training, both in terms of specific skills and broader training of the NTC type. If these are to be successful then the co-operation and support of trade unions and community organisations will have to be gained.
3. Short-term orientation courses for employment, on-the-job training, preferably combined with some formal education of the kind given, for example, in the British Youth Training Scheme. As in (2) above, trade union and community support will be critical.

Secondary school leavers with senior certificates

1. In the first place, what is needed here is an expansion of non-university, post-secondary education and training facilities in the shape of technikons, commercial colleges and 'community colleges'. These formal education facilities should also be used, for example, to offer science and mathematics to an acceptable standard to those who did not have these subjects in senior certificate or attained poor gradings. On a part-time basis these institutions should also be used to complement on-the-job training.

2. If the full potential of this group is to be released, the business world will have to take a much broader view of on-the-job training. It has to be remembered that 93% of successful African senior certificate candidates pass in the F (33-39%) category and that there are considerable gaps in their general education which need to be filled if on-the-job training is to be effective. In other words, industry and commerce will have to take responsibility for further education as well as the training specific to their needs.

3. Apart from the use of formal institutions, private agencies and in-company educational programmes, there will be a place (if the numbers involved are to be reached) for the use of distance teaching, backed up by local tutorial centres. However, distance teaching programmes are effective only when first-rate learning materials (backed up by newspapers, radio, TV, videos, etc) are made available at minimum cost, and where the motivation of the individual learner can be sustained.

It is to the youth and young adults in this broad group that the private sector should give priority in terms of funding, human resources and innovative thinking. It is in this area that it has to get involved in education as well as training, not only in non-formal programmes but in funding and supporting formal, non-university post-secondary institutions. It will have to play the major part in funding these initiatives, but will need state support in 'clearing the decks' for action. It will also have to involve community organisations and trade unions in the overall planning.

The time is ripe for this. In a whole range of political organisations the call is beginning to go out for the development of a learning culture in South Africa to repair the damage of the last 15 years. There will have to be a large measure of individual effort and commitment from the participants in the programmes; without this, success is not possible. Everyone will have to accept the risks that go along with any endeavour of this kind, and accept also that there are going to be failures as well as successes. There are no guarantees in education; it is a high risk business. But not to do anything and to be paralysed by the size of the problem carries much higher risks.

Those who are not literate and numerate

1. There is only one long-term solution for preventing the size of this group from growing larger each year, and that is compulsory, free primary schooling of good quality and relevance. This is the responsibility of the state and should be its first priority under any new educational dispensation.

2. In the short and medium term the attainment of basic education by those who did not go to school or dropped out prematurely will not be possible for the five to six million (conservatively estimated) in this group. Many will be too old, many have had to survive without it for so long that they will continue to do so, some will not have access to programmes and others will lack the strong motivation that is necessary for an adult to achieve literacy and numeracy, and sustain them. While making literacy programmes open to everyone it would be wise to concentrate resources and effort upon the youthful illiterates, up to about the age of 30.

World-wide, literacy has proved to be one of the most difficult social and educational issues to deal with, but at last the evidence seems to show that the turning point has been reached and numbers are no longer growing. Experience also shows that there are two major areas in which success is possible: the work situation, and where there are strong, cohesive communities, in which churches and national political organisations play a decisive role.

3. In the work situation it is employers and trade unions that will have to take primary responsibility for 'basic education' programmes, with some recognition from the state in the form of grants. An immediate step that needs to be taken is for business to use its clout to pressurise the state into recognising 'basic education' for grant purposes as a necessary foundation for skills training. This could be done under existing legislation.

In the community situation, churches and private agencies funded by foundations, trusts and the private sector in general, are likely to be much more effective than the state.

Primary school leavers and secondary school drop-outs

1. In the short and medium term, until compulsory primary schooling begins to 'turn the situation around', this group would not have as high a priority as the others in educational terms. However, it would become of increasing importance in the long term as the numbers of youngsters completing primary schooling increased. A working alternative to the conventional secondary school has to be found, and it will probably be found in a combination of work experience and further education and training. Some kind of formal system, as in Germany for example, where the private sector (providing the work experience) and the state are involved in a co-operative effort, will be the most effective in the long term.
2. While not carrying the highest priority in educational terms in the short and medium future, nevertheless this group carries very high social priority. It is the major group to which the state will have to give its attention immediately if there is not to be even greater alienation than already exists. It is difficult to establish but it probably has the highest rate of unemployment. It is pervaded by a sense of failure. It has nothing to lose. Violence is close to the surface, and the majority has no wish to return to school. If learning is to be re-established it will have to be in a completely different environment, probably one of work under fairly disciplined conditions. It will be important therefore, for South Africa, once a new government is in place, to experiment with a variety of programmes of the 'youth service', 'youth brigade', 'land service', 'conservation corps', etc, type, in order to establish which are ac-

ceptable and effective and could be applied on a larger scale.

International experience suggests that:

♦ Youth movements, while making a statistically small contribution to the solution of youth unemployment, can teach certain high-demand urban skills. They are less successful in relation to rural development.

♦ Older, politically aware youth make the most exacting demands and are the least amenable to discipline. Movements are much more successful with primary school leavers.

♦ It is not effective in most cases to appeal alone to the idealism of youth; the programmes must be seen to lead to employment and better earnings. This is the only way to counteract a tendency to low motivation and low-class stigma.

♦ The most effective programmes and movements have well-trained and well-paid instructors who provide good role models for trainees to follow. Trainees should spend at least two years in the programme. In such cases the costs are higher than in the formal school situation. Programmes of this kind cannot be run cheaply.

♦ Movements and programmes are much more successful at teaching skills than in changing attitudes. They can produce disciplined trainees, good party members and good soldiers, but are much less successful in producing good citizens for a democratic state.

♦ Only the state, sometimes with the help of considerable overseas funding, is able to cope with the requirements of such movements/programmes and make available the resources, departmental support, etc, and fit them in to the national development plan.

The programmes that have shown success have satisfied most of the following requirements:

♦ Adequate funding and resources, well-trained staff, full support from government and relevant departments.

♦ A combination of vocational skills training with an ideology of 'nation building', together with some continuation of the trainee's general education.

♦ The authority structure within the movement is crucial, as maximum use must be made of group participation, peer group solidarity and group support and co-operation if morale is to be raised, motivation strengthened and self-image and self-reliance improved.

♦ Participation should be voluntary if possible, and it appears that selection procedures are critical. Community organisations should be involved in this. Careful attention should be given to the age of applicants, and older trainees should be accepted only if they show ideal leadership qualities.

♦ Any tendency to emphasise 'academic' learning and to make the movement/programme look and act like a school should be resisted very firmly. The strength of the more effective organisations is that they are not schools. By providing adequate food, accommodation, clothing and health together with an atmosphere of competence and 'learning by doing' – a kind of apprenticeship – they provide a new kind of learning for those for whom schooling generally meant failure. If trainees can produce as well as learn this also strengthens motivation.

♦ While examinations should be 'played down' and cumulative assessment of practical ability encouraged, it will be critical to develop some form of certification when the trainee leaves, and these certificates must be accepted by employing bodies. The one thing above all others that movements/programmes have to achieve is 'to make good' previous failure. If they do not they will not survive.

♦ Militarisation should be resisted.

Summing up

In this brief review of the issues surrounding education and 'marginalised youth' two broad areas of concern have emerged:
1. the direct interface between work and schooling; and
2. the more complex relationship of those not in school, not employed, and the world of work.

The first is largely (but by no means entirely) a state responsibility. The second is largely (but by no means entirely) the responsibility of the individual, non-governmental organisations, and particularly the business sector.

In the first, the kinds of policy issues that have emerged have had to do with, for example, the provision of schooling facilities, such as introduction of compulsory primary schooling; the restructuring of secondary schooling (in which the private sector will have to make a contribution); the issue of quality, and how to achieve this, with the teacher and learning materials at the heart of this; the issue of relevance, which is largely a curriculum question, so that curriculum policy becomes perhaps the major issue in the direct interface between work and school.

In the second, a much more complex set of issues has emerged, in which the social, economic and political implications are even more powerful than in the first area of schooling. These issues have to do with such matters as the rehabilitation and reintegration into society and employment of a 'lost generation' of youth and young adults; policies and strategies for programmes of basic education (literacy and numeracy); effective distance teaching approaches and methods; on-the-job 'education' as well as training; on-the-job training together with education in formal institutions; re-directing and re-training youth towards science and, the most difficult of all, creating employment for young people that the formal sector cannot absorb, through some form of national service in which work and further education and training can be combined.

None of this will be easy, nor can everything be done at the same time, but as time runs out on us something has to be seen to be done while the political process is taking its course, as well as after a new constitutional agreement has been achieved. The state, which is in something of an interregnum, is not in a good position to do this. The business sector, with community and trade union support and agreement, and with the 'will' to do so, could be.

Table 1: Categories of youth according to educational status

Group A	
Sub-group 1	**Sub-group 2**
No schooling at all. In 1988 there were about two million young people between ages seven and 16 who were not in school at all. However, this does not mean that all of them have no schooling.	Dropped out of school before completing Standard 4. These can be regarded as not literate or numerate. In numbers this is the biggest group: each year one third of a million youngsters are added to the conservative estimate of five to six million non-literate South Africans.
Group B	
Sub-group 1	**Sub-group 2**
Those who completed primary school but went no further.	Those who dropped out in secondary school. In total, this group amounts to 225 000 school leavers per year.
Group C	
Sub-group 1	**Sub-group 2**
Those who passed senior certificate, but failed to gain matriculation exemption. Those with a matriculation certificate have been omitted from Group C in the hope that they have a better chance. In practice many of them require further support and re-training, because of the low quality of their results and the absence of science and mathematics.	Those who failed to gain any certificate in the final secondary school leaving examination. This group is increasing by 125 000 per year. From 1980 to 1989, 521 370 pupils completed secondary schooling with a matric or senior certificate, but about 515 000 had to leave without any formal certificate, having failed the final examination.

4

Marginalised Youth and Unemployment

Rory Riordan

Unemployment is a worldwide phenomenon. It is particularly serious in third world countries where it has assumed crisis proportions. South Africa is no exception. In a recent countrywide survey conducted by Human Sciences Research Council (HSRC) researchers, results showed that all four population groups (white, African, coloured and Asian) collectively identified unemployment (or the need for employment opportunities) as a major problem area.[1]
– E P Whittle

In surveys conducted in Port Elizabeth's African and coloured population groups at the height of the 1987/1988 state of emergency, each population group listed 'unemployment and lack of jobs' as the biggest problem area facing African and coloured people in Port Elizabeth.

A survey conducted by Professor Valerie Moller on black youth (aged 16 to 24) in selected townships in Johannesburg, Cape Town and Durban, showed that unemployment was rated as the second largest problem for young people, behind only teenage pregnancy.[2]

Thus, any study of marginalised South African youth must begin with an assessment of unemployment, and employment prospects.

This article examines the problem of unemployment in South Africa, showing that unemployment, underemployment and broken contact with employment are definitive characteristics of the concept of 'marginalised youth'. It provides a brief background of some world trends in unemployment and then surveys unemployment trends in South Africa. Port Elizabeth is treated as a case study. The chapter ends with some suggestions on how to address the problem of unemployment.

For the purposes of this discussion, the 'youth' are defined as those ranging from adolescence to young adulthood who are not yet exercising responsibility as head of a household. The age range is from about 13 to 29 and covers three categories – adolescence, post-adolescence, and young adults.

'Marginalised' people are those who now, and in the future South Africa, will be difficult to incorporate into society's educational, economic, social and political institutions.

There are many definitions of employment and the discussion of what constitutes employment and unemployment is an area of study in itself. I use the definition provided by the International Labour Organisation (ILO), not because it is without problems, but because it is a standard definition used by statistics bureaux in most countries. The ILO definition is used by the Central Statistical Services (CSS) in South Africa's Current Population Surveys. It is as follows:[3]

The employed are persons 15 years and older, who during the so-called reference week (that is the seven days preceding the interview) worked for five or more hours for wage or salary or for profit or family gain, in cash or in kind. Persons who had commenced work in their present job and who were temporarily absent from work during the reference week, and worked for less than five hours but still had a formal job attachment, are also included.

The unemployed are persons who, being 15 years and older

a) are not in paid employment or self-employed as defined above;

b) were available for paid employment or self-employment during the reference week (the seven days preceding the interview); and

c) took specific steps during the four weeks preceding the interview to find paid employment or self-employment; or

d) had the desire to work and to take up employment or self-employment.

The non-economically active population consists of all persons, irrespective of age who, at the time of the survey, were neither employed nor unemployed as defined above.

World trends in employment and unemployment

A few trends in world unemployment serve to put the South African unemployment issue into perspective.

During the past 20 years unemployment has increased in the major industrialised countries. Unemployment rates in these countries in 1987 were nearly three times as high as they were in 1970. For example Japan's unemployment rate in 1970 was 1%. By 1987 it had increased to 3,4%. West Germany's unemployment rate rose from 0,8% in 1970 to 8% in 1987 while that of Britain increased from 3% to 13% in the same years. The only country which did not show a consistent increase in its unemployment rate was the United States where the rate rose from 4,8% in 1970, peaked to 9,5% in 1982 and by 1987 dropped to 6,8%.

Unemployment rates in the world's developing, and poorer, countries are more difficult to quantify. Figures are not as reliably kept, and a general rule applies here: the lower the income economy, the greater the percentage of the workforce involved in agriculture. Of the World Bank's 39 'low income economies' in 1980, an average of 72% of the workforce was employed in agriculture, as opposed to 7% in the 19 'industrial market economies.'[4] Employment rates in agriculture are very difficult to quantify accurately, particularly in peasant agriculture, and this goes a long way to explain why there is such a paucity of statistical information on this issue.

Nevertheless, indications are that unemployment is an integral part of the crisis facing developing countries, as Robert NcNamara, president of the World Bank in the 1970s pointed out:

> *The cities are filling up and urban unemployment steadily grows... (T)he 'marginal men', the wretched strugglers for survival on the fringes of farms and cities, may already number half a billion. By 1980 they will surpass a billion, and by 1990 two billion. Can we imagine any human order surviving with so gross a mass of misery piling up at its base?*

One of the main causes of unemployment in highly industrialised countries has been the decline in manufacturing employment due to increased capital intensity through the use of machines and computers. Employment in manufacturing has declined though manufacturing output has been sustained or increased. For example, manufacturing production in the United States rose by almost 40% between 1973 and 1985 but today there are five million fewer people employed in blue-collar work in American manufacturing industry than there were in 1975.

The same patterns are evident in Japan and Britain. In Britain, the Index of Output of total manufacturing was almost identical in 1985 to 1975.[5] Yet manufacturing employment had come down by nearly a third.[6]

When growth in employment has taken place, it has been in white collar jobs. For example, Drucker notes that in the last 12 years total employment in the United States grew faster than at any time in the peacetime history of any country — from 82 to 110 million between 1973 and 1985, or by a full one-third. The entire growth, however, was in non-manufacturing, and especially white collar, jobs in knowledge-intensive (eg computer) and service (eg food chains and tourism) industries.

Developed market economies have been buffeted by contradictory aggregate demand shocks in the 1980s. Some were intended. For example, in a bid to lower inflation rates most Western European countries and Japan matched the tight monetary policies of the United States in the early 1980s. Japan and Western European countries also engaged in prolonged fiscal tightening. Since 1982, however, the USA has followed a strongly expansionary fiscal policy.

This has helped the USA achieve a reduction in unemployment, while the lack of a strong fiscal policy in the other developed market economies helped their unemployment rates to rise.

The economic policies of the world's countries have been profoundly affected by the two major recessions experienced by the industrial economies in 1957 and 1982 — the worst since the 1930s. These led to commodity price rises in the 1970s, notably the oil price rises of 1973/4 and 1979/80; exchange rate shocks, with the dollar falling sharply in the 1970s, and then rising sharply in the 1980s; and inflation and interest rate shocks, with inflation spiralling in the 1970s.

Paul Klugman[7] notes that most countries have responded to these external shocks by action aimed at improving endangered trade balances. The policies have inevitably been aimed at reducing domestic spending, and thereby reducing the demand for imports. But this has also reduced the demand for local goods, thereby fuelling unemployment.

The collapse of commodity prices in the 1980s has been a major cause of growing unemployment in third world countries. Most of these countries earn the bulk of their precious foreign exchange through the sale of base minerals, or other primary commodities, to the developed industrial economies. By early 1986, Drucker writes, 'raw material prices were at their lowest levels in recorded history in relation to the prices of manufactured goods and services – in general as low as in the depth of the Great Depression.'[8]

The main reason for this dramatic fall in commodity prices is shrinking demand – 'The amount of industrial raw materials needed for one unit of industrial production is now no more than two-fifths of what it was in 1900.' Zambia is a classic example of an economy affected by shrinking demand for its major primary commodity – 50 kilograms of fibre glass cable transmits at least as many telephone messages as a thousand kilograms of copper wire. The consequences of this have been disastrous and Zambia has almost no foreign exchange today.

Korea is often cited as a shining example for less developed countries because it has managed to reduce its unemployment rate. Korea's unemployment rate dropped from 7,8% in 1960/65, to 4,2% in 1981/84.[9] This is the result of outstanding GNP growth, which in turn is based on incredible growth in the export of manufactured goods. The Korean example shows that a dramatic growth in manufacturing exports can shift a less developed country with considerable unemployment into a developed nation with very little unemployment. The example is particularly instructive for South Africa, although there appear to be many reasons why it will be very difficult to adapt 'the Korean model' to South African conditions.

Unemployment trends in South Africa

Charles Simkins, in a now-famous paper,[10] asserted that African unemployment nationwide was much higher than previous calculations for the mid-1970s (4%-8%). He argued that it was persistent and seemed to hold at between 19% and 22,4% between 1961 and 1977. African unemployment appeared for the first time to be endemic, largely unresponsive to cyclical swings in the economy, and at a much higher level than previously envisaged.

Simkins' controversial paper stimulated a search for better ways of obtaining reliable statistics and increased interest in research on unemployment calculations.[11] As a result of Simkins' work, the Central Statistical Services began collecting data on unemployment particularly amongst Africans. Even conservative organisations were willing to concede that, by 1982, the percentage of the workforce without formal employment opportunities had reached 31,7%.[12]

The number of formally unemployed has soared from 22% in 1970 to 30% in 1980 then to 40% in 1989. This supports the observation by the President's Council that the unemployment problem is of a structural nature and that it can be alleviated but not solved by a cyclical upswing in the economy.[13]

Rising unemployment coincides with and is partly a consequence of the decreasing labour absorptive capacity of the economy. Development Bank figures show that in the late 1960s there were 145 000 jobs created every year as compared to 45 000 between 1985 and 1989:

During the period 1965 to 1970, almost 75% of the average annual number of entrants to the labour market were accommodated by the formal economic sector. This percentage decreased continuously from then and reached 35% and 22% during the periods 1975-1980 and 1980-1985, respectively. There was a further dramatic decrease in the absorption capacity of the formal sector to only

*12,5% during the period 1985/1989. The implication is that
only 125 out of almost 1 000 new entrants per day to the
labour market could be accommodated as full-term
employees during the past four years.*[14]

The Development Bank research[15] shows that almost 85%
of the unemployed in South Africa are from the black
population. The research also reveals huge regional disparities in employment levels. The National Manpower
Commission[16] has noted that black unemployment dis-
plays only a mild sensitivity to the business cycle, which
confirms the predominantly structural nature of the problem. Wilson and Ramphele have argued that the primary
reasons for the slow-down in the rate of growth of employment since the late 1960s lies beyond Southern Africa, in
the wider global economy.[17]

The rate of growth in various sectors of the South African economy has declined continuously since the 1960s.
Wilson and Ramphele comment on this decreasing rate of
employment as follows:

*In agriculture the rate slowed down earlier but became ne-
gative in the mid-1960s. In the major, private, 'non-agricul-
tural' sectors, the rate fell sharply, well below the population growth rate, after 1975. A similar pattern was found in
the finance and service sectors. Thus, so long as the
growth of employment in the economy as a whole lies
below the rate of growth of population, the level of
unemployment must go on rising inexorably...*[18]

Between 1970 and 1976, total employment in full-time
agriculture fell by about 150 000 full-time jobs. Mechanisation, growth in the use of tractors, combine harvesters and
grain silos caused a drop of 50% in the need for seasonal
workers in the maize areas of the Western Transvaal. This
substitution was for 'best-practice techniques', and not because capital was cheap and labour expensive.

The decline in the rate of growth of employment

coincided with a rapidly increasing demand for wage labour among black South Africans. This increased demand is the result of what has been described by Thomas[19] as South Africa's 'demographic transition.' He outlines four main factors which have led to this transition:

♦ A high birth-rate combined with a dropping mortality rate, and a high school drop-out rate, have put many black youngsters, poorly educated, into the employment market.

♦ African migrant labourers, who previously retired after 20 years of work, now have to work through to retirement age.

♦ African women are being driven into the work market.

♦ Urbanisation, accompanied by changing consumption patterns, rising expectations and a shift to core families, places virtually all members of the family under pressure to earn an income.

The combination of the decline in the rate of growth of employment and the increase in the numbers of black South Africans seeking jobs resulted in a huge increase in African unemployment.

Other population groups have been sheltered from unemployment by apartheid policy which gave them better access to secondary and tertiary education and enabled them to urbanise earlier, and by military service and lower fertility rates.

Initially, the waves of African urbanisation of the 1980s have caused a growth in squatter settlements, and visibly higher unemployment in the towns. But the longer-term effects may be the opposite – the stimulation of economic activities in the metropolitan areas and the easing of land pressures and facilitation of land reform.

The President's Council[20] emphasised a number of 'limiting factors' influencing the ability of the South African economy to create employment: inadequate education and training, being the result of bantu education; flight of foreign capital due to political and social tension; savings and capital formation, which are too low to generate adequate investment capital; and sanctions, which undoubtedly helped to constrict the economy and exacerbated the problem of job creation, especially in the less skilled categories.

Port Elizabeth – a case study

A pioneering report by David Gilmour and Andre Roux,[21] published in 1984, uncovered an African unemployment rate of 38% for Port Elizabeth. This was, at the time, astronomical by major city standards in South Africa. Furthermore, the onset of mass unemployment had appeared quite recently, with only 20% to 30% of Gilmour and Roux's sample having been unemployed for more than two years.

By August 1985 the Department of Manpower had 25% of the total African population in Port Elizabeth registered as unemployed, and the first of the now-annual Vista University surveys, conducted in June 1985, showed that 56% of African men between 16 and 55 years, and African women between 16 and 60 years, were unable to find any sort of work.[22] Vista University believed that an additional 25% of all employed adults were either underemployed or in part-time employment. Further Vista surveys have shown that the unemployed percentage dropped below 50% in 1987, and rose again to above 50% in 1988. Whatever the exact percentage, there can be no doubt that Port Elizabeth, like most other third world cities, is experiencing an unemployment crisis.

Young women feature prominently amongst the unemployed. Central Statistical Services figures show that, of the total unemployed, 56% are female, and 55% are under 29 years of age. The female statistic is consistent with Vista's finding that 54% of all unemployed in Port Elizabeth were female.

Shack community studies reveal more stark statistics. Planact found 57% of all females unemployed in Langa as opposed to 40% of males,[23] and a Human Rights Trust (HRT) survey in Silvertown found 58% of all unemployed to be female. Of this sample of unemployed, 53% were under 30 years of age.

In Silvertown, the HRT survey found that of those in employment, 80% were male and only 20% female. Of the females employed, 74% were domestic workers with only 26% of women in employment in hourly-paid jobs. There was a further masking statistic with regard to female unemployment: four times as many women claimed to be 'housewives' as were in employment. In some cases, a 'housewife' would be the only adult in a household containing many children. This suggests that the category of 'housewife' was masking a higher female unemployment statistic in this shack community.[24]

Unemployment appears to be more common in poor households, implying that those in wealthier households can finance longer job searches, and have better introductory contact in the workplace. Gilmour and Roux found that 60% of all unemployed come from households living under the Household Subsistence Level (HSL) and that 78% of employed males come from households above this level. The Human Rights Trust Silvertown survey found that 90% of all unemployed were in households under the HSL, whereas 51% of all in employment were in households above the HSL.

More recent Vista University research[25] confirms the unemployment rate at 47% of the economically active African population (those of working age minus those preferring not to work, ie housewives, students, disabled and those not fit to work). This implies that '112 700 black people in the Port Elizabeth/Uitenhage Municipal Area were unemployed in June 1989.'

The Vista research revealed that unemployment was highest among those in the 21-35 year age bracket. Young women constituted the majority of the unemployed: 'Of the total number of unemployed Africans, 68,8% were 35 years of age or younger. This amounts to 77 538 people, of whom approximately 31 325 are male, and 46 213 are female'.

Unemployment was, by 1989, plainly a long-term phenomenon, with 57% of unemployed Africans having been unemployed for two years or longer. Of those aged 35 years and younger, 45% had been unemployed for two years or longer.

The research also revealed that education did not increase employment prospects. Gilmour and Roux juxtaposed two of their findings: that employed men are only slightly better educated than unemployed men, and that unemployed females are marginally better educated than their employed counterparts; and that, for unskilled and semi-skilled jobs (which Simkins and Hindson have shown to be 80% of all jobs held by Africans), education has little effect on recruitment chances. Some 90% of unskilled jobs go to workers with Standard 6 or less, and 93% of all semi-skilled jobs to workers with Standard 8 or less, Gilmour and Roux found. As there is at most a one in three chance of any African school-leaver gaining non-manual employment, it would appear that expectations of education leading to job placement are sadly out of line.

Possibly, however, there is a hope for those Africans who can climb right up the ladder of education. Planact found that, of all Langa shack-dwellers with Standard 9 or higher, 72% were in employment and only 28% were not.

The Vista work confirms this trend. The Vista research notes that 53% of unemployed Africans in Port Elizabeth/Uitenhage have school qualifications varying between Standard 6 and Standard 10. Of those 35 years old and younger, 57% of the unemployed had a Standard 6-10 qualification.

Gilmour and Roux came to two conclusions: that the unemployed are most likely to be female, junior members of households, single and childless; and that of those in the job queue, the profile of the person most likely to be employed is of a middle-aged male who had worked before and had proof of it, and had technical training and had proof of that.

In addition, the unemployed come from poorer households, often in shack areas; and that the figures for female unemployed might be doubly masked, firstly by incorrect self-evaluation of a 'housewife,' and secondly by high female employment in domestic service, an occupation

with a wage per hour rate closer to slavery than employment.

Gilmour and Roux found that nearly 90% of
unemployed males searched for employment weekly; 82%
of the Human Rights Trust's Silvertown sample had been
searching for work daily; and 63% of this sample had been
searching unsuccessfully for between ten months and two
years. All went to both labour bureaux and factories, and
46% went to homes as well.

Asked if there was any hope in searching for jobs,
work-seekers of Silvertown had no illusions: only 2% believed they would get work in the next month, 3% within
the next three months, and 19% within the next year.
About half of the group replied 'don't know' to the question, and kept plodding on.

The following factors account for the high level of unemployment in Port Elizabeth:

Demographic pressures, including urbanisation: Population figures, particularly for South Africa's African population, are uniformly unreliable. We must nevertheless use
them as a guide.

Between the 1970 and the 1985 census, the African
population of Port Elizabeth/Uitenhage increased by 229%,
from 205 700 in 1970 to 471 300 in 1985. For the five
years between 1980 and 1985, it increased by 7% per
annum, compounded. Natural growth is expected to tie in
with the national average of about 3% – the remaining 4%
must be accounted for by urbanisation. For the period
1965 to 1985, Korea increased manufactured exports from
$175 million to $292 435 million and thereby dropped unemployment from 5,5% to 4,2%. Korea had a population
growth of 1,7% over this period. This implies that it is virtually impossible to create jobs in a formal sector to ac-
commodate a population growth of 7% per annum.

Low levels of education: The education level of the
African community would appear to be too low for it to
generate significant formal employment from within its own
resources. As of the 1985 census there were 237 black
graduates in Port Elizabeth, and about 2 500 people with

diplomas and either Standard 9 or 10. The quality of black education can be described at best as lacking, and at worst hardly of the quality to generate entrepreneurs or businesspeople in numbers.

Lack of growth in manufacturing employment: Mechanisation and computerisation have not as yet had a significant impact on reducing the labour component in Port Elizabeth's manufacturing industry. Part of the cause might be the historical unwillingness of the local foreign-owned motor industry to invest heavily in capital intensive machinery because of the threat of disinvestment.

There has, nevertheless, been a significant migration of the footwear industry from Port Elizabeth to Natal. Peter Morum, the president of the Midland Chamber of Industries, estimated that this cost Port Elizabeth 10 000 jobs. Port Elizabeth's share of the nation's footwear production has dropped from 24% to about 9%.

Disinvestment: Disinvestment has cost Port Elizabeth the Ford Motor Company, which merged with Anglo's Samcor and relocated to Pretoria. Reuben Els, Samcor's public affairs manager, revealed that 5 000 Ford workers lost their jobs in this move, and the ripple effect on subsidiary industry must have been as severe.

Lack of demand: Lack of demand in the South African economy has been caused by the prolonged recession of the 1980s, and the fiscal demand-reduction policies pursued by the authorities in their fight with inflation and balance of payments crises. This lack of demand has resulted in a profound weakness in the vehicle and consumer goods markets, affecting Port Elizabeth particularly harshly.

Lack of development of 'knowledge' and service industries in the Eastern Cape: While Port Elizabeth can claim a few capable and expanding pharmaceutical companies, it has not participated in the development of the South African electronics or computer industries. Possible causes could include the fact that Port Elizabeth's universities have only recently opened (UPE 1965, Vista 1979). Consequently the number of graduates in the area is low

(7 594 graduates according to the 1985 Census).

The area has seen the development of few service industries, the major source of job growth in the USA. Tourism is little developed and the area has difficulty competing with the scenic attractions of the Western Cape or the game farms and casino resorts of the Transvaal. In the absence of a strong tourist industry, it is unlikely that hotels, restaurants and related services will develop.

Low level of manufacturing exports: Manufacturing exports from the area are comparatively underdeveloped, and this situation is unlikely to change until sanctions are fully lifted.

Nature of agricultural production: Agriculture in the area is mostly wool and mohair, and as such is not as labour intensive as the Western Cape's fruit industry. Thus the agricultural hinterland will continue to send people to the cities, rather than offer them jobs.

The unemployment crisis, which is of global, national and regional magnitude, clearly has to be tackled on a broad front.

Implementing a job creation strategy

Over the past decade, there has been a shift away from state employment, cyclical stabilisation and old-style regional job creation towards greater market efficiency, an improvement in the quality of labour, the stimulation of entrepreneurship and small business, and greater willingness to accept urbanisation.

Recently, this emphasis has shifted further towards mobilising greater capital supply, and sector or industry-specific structural adjustments which have the potential for more job creation in the longer term.

Three areas given the lowest priority so far involve the dampening of the quantitative labour supply, which is essentially a long-term strategy; ameliorative and redistributive policies, which are politically and financially difficult to pursue; and local or community-based job creation efforts, which depend on local rather than state policy initiatives.

Against this background of changing policies and high levels of unemployment we have to ask what can be done to increase the effectiveness of policies. The following areas merit careful consideration:

First, we need *the political will of policy makers* as opposed to lip service to achieve significant results. Given the present structure of power in South Africa, those directly affected by unemployment play, at best, only a subordinate role in decision making. Dominant interest groups focus mostly on policies which only indirectly support job creation. Those directly concerned with unemployment have little leverage in the decision-making process.

With the changing balance of political power in South Africa we should, however, expect the thrust of such policies to change.

A second precondition for more effective policy implementation is *the close monitoring of present policies on their success in job creation.* The task seems vast, since we do not actually know which policies will succeed in stimulating employment. Besides, more detailed measurements of employment are required with respect to regions, towns, economic sectors, industries and community areas.

A third dimension follows directly from the above – *the need for explicit quantitative targetting of job creation policies.* National employment targets related to the expected growth in the labour force should be set, as well as indicative targets for different regions, sectors, industries and local communities. This does not suggest that job creation policies can be designed to achieve any chosen target, but it forces policy makers to think carefully about their promises.

A fourth dimension concerns the *education of the public about feasible and/or effective job creation policies.* In a polarised, semi-developed society like South Africa it will often be difficult to mobilise support for specific policies, especially if there is no guaranteed short-term net employment increase. The dilemma becomes even greater if longer-term policies (like wage restraint) are seen to have a detrimental short-term or distributional effect on some interest groups – particularly those more exposed to short-term unemployment.

Greater policy efficiency will depend largely on *the structuring of particular policies.* For example, the Small Business Development Corporation is constantly reviewing the effectiveness of alternative ways of assisting informal sector job creation and job maintenance. And the debate about practical ways of work-sharing and/or reducing the work week of those employed (to benefit the unemployed) has hardly started in this country.

Finally, far more attention must be paid to *the employment process at the level of macro-economic data analysis and government budgets.* Most short-term economic forecasts contain virtually no employment projections, while the authoritative Reserve Bank bulletin pays only marginal attention to employment trends.

These proposals for a more effective job creation strategy indicate the need for a broad-based job creation movement in South Africa. The need for such a movement does not contradict the undeniable progress that has already been made in job creation so far. It merely suggests that there is enormous scope for improvement. Central government, regional and local authorities, organised business, big business, consumer organisations, organised labour, the small business sector, community groups and voluntary organisations all have an important role to play in initiating such a movement.

The co-ordinating role in such a national employment drive might fall upon the National Manpower Commission or the Department of Manpower, although both are probably too closely tied to government to be able to ensure bi-partisan support. It might thus be necessary to create an umbrella body broad enough in its composition to represent all those interests, yet flexible and streamlined enough to play the role of an efficient co-ordinating secretariat, rather than adding yet another bureaucratic layer to society.

Such a secretariat, supported by the different bodies mentioned above, would have to draw up a medium-term employment framework with broad, overall targets for job creation. All relevant policy-making bodies would have to co-operate to set annual targets linked to different policy areas. The annual revision of these targets, based on detailed monitoring of the job creation process and ongoing policy adjustments, would be the symbolic focal point of such a movement, where development is measured in terms of employment and job creation.

There is the need for a study of the size, location of, regional differences in, and existence of, 'marginalised youth'.

This study should combine statistical/demographic information with attitudinal information. The objective of the survey should be to provide information that would help to frame a coherent policy for a post-apartheid government.

Public sector works projects are an effective means of job creation. Ligthelm and Kritzinger-van Niekerk have provided guidelines for restructuring expenditure programmes of the public sector. To ensure that they are effective, programmes should

♦ be aimed at addressing structural unemployment, poverty and a more equal distribution of wealth while increasing the growth capacity of the economy;

♦ not be regarded as separate employment creation exercises, in addition to existing expenditure programmes;

♦ incorporate appropriate technology (in South Africa, capital intensive projects should only be used when labour intensive methods are not efficient);

♦ use available local human and physical resources and institutions, and involve local communities.

One of the spectacular successes of recent years has been the growth of the informal sector in the South African economy. Based on CSS statistics, Servaas van der Berg has calculated that 'it appears that the effect of informal sector activity is to increase black per capita income by 50%'.[26] However, Van der Berg's figures show that only in the transport section (mostly black taxis) is a wage paid that is above the Household Subsistence Level.

There is some evidence to suggest that Port

Elizabeth's fledgling African informal sector may not be generating any considerable number of well-paid jobs. Research by Professors du Plessis and Levin of Vista University[27] showed low earnings in the informal sector, averaging R305 per month, and approximating subsistence incomes. The number of employees per enterprise was less than two – the owner, plus and average of only 0,6 others. This suggests that the employment generating potential of enterprises in this sector is restricted.

Similar problems were faced by all informal enterprises – obtaining short and long-term loans, accommodation, poor infrastructure and legal restrictions. Thus the much vaunted informal sector, when in the hands of a community with very low levels of education and commercial experience, may not be a significant generator of employment after all.

While informal sector activities are fundamentally valuable in defeating welfare mentality and in creating self--reliance, we must not be sanguine about work conditions therein. The goal remains a good formal sector job for each aspirant worker.

Economic growth is a *sine qua non* for poverty alleviation and job creation, and must be a foundation for economic policy. Thomas[28] notes that, in contrast to real growth rates of about 6% in the 1960s, and 3% in the 1970s, growth in the South African economy dropped to less than 2% in the 1980s (with negative growth thus far in the 1990s). This affected employment growth: 'Official statistics on GDP growth and total employment in the formal economy follow similar trends: a decline in the real growth is matched by a less expansive – if not negative – formal sector employment trend.'

Nobody should convince themselves that the problem of marginalised youth, involving as it does the above social disasters, will easily pass. It will probably be with us forever. Hopefully this paper, and the others in this collection, can go somewhere to beginning a set of solutions.

Notes

1. EP Whittle, 'Findings of a survey of problem areas in South African society', HSRC, Pretoria, 1990.
2. Rory Riordan, 'Township Political Loyalties', *Monitor*, June 1988.
3. From 'explanatory notes' as used in 'Current Population Surveys', 1991 Census (PO342).
4. Table 31, 'Labour Force', *World Development Report*, 1988, The World Bank, Washington, 1986, 282-283.
5. Peter Donaldson and John Farquhar, *Understanding the British Economy*, London, 1988, 57.
6. Donaldson and Farquhar, *Understanding the British Economy*, 13.
7. Paul Klugman, 'External Shocks and Domestic Policy Responses', in Rudiger Dornbusch and F Leslie Helmers (eds), *The Open Economy*, The World Bank, Washington, 1988, 542.
8. Peter Drucker, 'Dramatic Shifts in the Global Economy' , *Foreign Affairs*, Spring 1986.
9. Young-Chul Park, 'Korea', in R Dornbusch and F Helmers (eds), *The Open Economy*, The World Bank, 1988.
10. Charles Simkins, 'Measuring and predicting unemployment in South Africa, 1960-77', in C Simkins and C Clarke, *Structural Unemployment in South Africa*, University of Natal, Pietermaritzburg, 1978.
11. F Wilson and M Ramphele, *Uprooting Poverty. The South African Challenge,* Cape Town, 1990, 84.
12. President's Council, *Report of a Strategy for Employment Creation and Labour Intensive Development*, Government Printer, Pretoria, 1987, 11.
13. AA Ligthelm and L Kritzinger-van Niekerk, 'Unemployment: The role of the public sector in increasing the labour absorption capacity of the South African Economy', *Development Southern Africa*, 7(4), November 1990.
14. Ligthelm and Kritzinger-van Niekerk, 'Unemployment', 630.
15. Ligthelm and Kritzinger-van Niekerk, 'Unemployment', 633.
16. Ligthelm and Kritzinger-van Niekerk, 'Unemployment'.
17. Wilson and Ramphele, *Uprooting Poverty*, 243-244.
18. Wilson and Ramphele, *Uprooting Poverty*.
19. Wolfgang H Thomas, 'Unemployment and the job creation challenge', in Robert Schrire (ed), *Critical Choices for South Africa*, Cape Town, 1990, 250.
20. President's Council, *Report of a Strategy for Employment Creation*; Ronald Bethlehem, *Economics in a Revolutionary Society*, Johannesburg, 1988, 177.
21. David Gilmour and Andre Roux, 'Urban Black Unemployment and Education in the Eastern Cape', Carnegie Conference Paper No. 120, University of Cape Town, Cape Town, 1984.

22. M Levin and GS Horn, 'The Unemployment Rate of Blacks in the Port Elizabeth Metropole Area, 1987', Research Report No. 7, Vista University, August 1987.
23. Planact, *Langa. The case for upgrade*, Johannesburg, 1986.
24.Rory Riordan, 'The Ukuhleleleka of Port Elizabeth', *Monitor*, June 1988, 10.
25. Vista University, 'A Profile of Unemployed Blacks in the Port Elizabeth/Uitenhage Metropolitan Area', Port Elizabeth, 1989.
26. Servaas van der Berg, 'Shadow Boxing over Size', *Indicator*, 7(3), Winter 1990.
27. AP du Plessis and M Levin, 'The informal sector in selected residential areas of Port Elizabeth', *Development Southern Africa*, August 1988, 348.
28. Thomas, 'Unemployment and the job creation challenge', 256.